OCCASIONAL PAPER 183

Economic Reforms in Kazakhstan, Kyrgyz Republic, Tajikistan, Turkmenistan, and Uzbekistan

Emine Gürgen, Harry Snoek, Jon Craig, Jimmy McHugh,
Ivailo Izvorski, and Ron van Rooden

D1528973

INTERNATIONAL MONETARY FUND
Washington DC
1999

Production: IMF Graphics Section
Figures: Theodore F. Peters, Jr.
Typesetting: Alicia Etchebarne-Bourdin

Library of Congress Cataloging-in-Publication Data

Economic reforms in Kazakhstan, Kyrgyz Republic, Tajikistan, Turkmenistan, and Uzbekistan / Emine Gürgen . . . [et. al.]

     p.   cm. — (Occasional paper, ISSN 0251-6365; no. 183)
    Includes bibliographical references (p.   ).
    ISBN 1-55775-825-5

    1. Asia, Central—Economic policy. 2. Asia, Central—Economic condi-
tions. I. Gürgen, Emine. II. Series: Occasional paper (International Monetary
Fund); no. 183.
HC420.3.E27 1999
338.958—dc21   99-33742
                                               CIP

Price: US$18.00
(US$15.00 to full-time faculty members and
students at universities and colleges)

Please send orders to:
International Monetary Fund, Publication Services
700 19th Street, N.W., Washington, D.C. 20431, U.S.A.
Tel.: (202) 623-7430   Telefax: (202) 623-7201
E-mail: publications@imf.org
Internet: http://www.imf.org

recycled paper

Contents

Tables

Figures

The following symbols have been used throughout this paper:

. . . to indicate that data are not available;

— to indicate that the figure is zero or less than half the final digit shown, or that the item does not exist;

– between years or months (for example, 1994–95 or January–June) to indicate the years or months covered, including the beginning and ending years or months;

/ between years (for example, 1994/95) to indicate a crop or fiscal (financial) year.

"Billion" means a thousand million.

Minor discrepancies between constituent figures and totals are due to rounding.

The term "country," as used in this paper, does not in all cases refer to a territorial entity that is a state as understood by international law and practice; the term also covers some territorial entities that are not states, but for which statistical data are maintained and provided internationally on a separate and independent basis.

Preface

This occasional paper provides an overview of the economic reform experiences of the Central Asian states of the former Soviet Union since their independence at the turn of the decade. The choice of countries—Kazakhstan, the Kyrgyz Republic, Tajikistan, Turkmenistan, and Uzbekistan—reflects not only a geographical grouping, but also similarities in the types of transition challenges faced by these countries, notwithstanding considerable variations in their sizes, ethnic compositions, resource endowments, and economic structures. The paper highlights these differences and the impact they may have had on the individual approaches to and progress with economic reforms, while also tracing some of the common threads that run through the transition experience of each country. In this fashion, it attempts to identify a number of key macroeconomic and structural areas where the slower reformers in the group might benefit from the experience of the faster reformers.

The paper was a collaborative project under the leadership of Emine Gürgen. Helpful suggestions were received from John Odling-Smee, Oleh Havrylyshyn, and Leif Hansen. In addition, the authors are indebted to several colleagues in the International Monetary Fund, notably Isaias Coelho, Jens Dalsgaard, Jan Mikkelsen, Johannes Mueller, and Richard Stern for their constructive comments; Sepideh Khazai for research assistance; and Helen John for secretarial work. Helen Chin of the External Relations Department edited the paper and coordinated its production for publication.

The contributions to the paper drew considerably on the work undertaken by the European II Department, in the context of discussions held with the governments of the countries reviewed, on the use of IMF resources and in conducting the annual Article IV consultations. However, the opinions expressed are solely those of the authors and do not necessarily reflect the opinions of the IMF staff, Executive Directors, or the country authorities.

I Overview

Emine Gürgen

At the outset of their transition to a market economy, the social and economic indicators in the Central Asian states of the former Soviet Union—Kazakhstan, the Kyrgyz Republic, Tajikistan, Turkmenistan, and Uzbekistan—generally fell short of the standards of the region as a whole. Notably, per capita incomes ranged from just over 50 percent (Tajikistan) to about 90 percent (Kazakhstan) of the Soviet Union average, while social indicators, such as life expectancy, infant mortality, health facilities, and housing conditions, were considerably worse in most cases. All five Central Asian states—landlocked and distant from world markets—depended heavily on an intricate Soviet system of trade routes and energy pipelines for essential input supplies and exports. Rich agricultural, mineral, and fuel resources of the region, though, made it a potentially attractive outlet for foreign investors. Following a long period of isolation and catering to the needs of the Soviet Union, these countries faced the tough challenge of how to exploit more effectively their natural resources to improve living standards, while simultaneously introducing the systemic changes needed to achieve a market framework and to integrate their economies with the rest of the world.

The Central Asian states have gone part of the way toward meeting this challenge since their independence at the beginning of the decade. There is visible evidence of progress by all five countries toward decentralizing their economies, expanding international links, and intensifying efforts to diversify and increase production and trade. Comparisons with other transforming economies inside and outside of the region, however, indicate that considerable ground still needs to be covered in a number of areas. Notably, the private sector's share constitutes less than one-half of economic activity in most of the Central Asian states, and banking systems (except in the Kyrgyz Republic) continue to be heavily state controlled, while per capita foreign direct investment into the region (except for Kazakhstan) remains relatively low. Also, a set of transition indicators, developed by the European Bank for Reconstruction and Development (EBRD) to measure progress with privatization, enterprise restructuring, price, trade, and financial sector reforms in transition economies, indicates a mixed performance by the Central Asian states, with considerable catching up needed in Tajikistan, Turkmenistan, and Uzbekistan (Table 1.1).

The pace and intensity of reforms have varied widely across the countries in the group. While differences in natural resource endowments, economic structures, and sociocultural factors undoubtedly influenced attitudes toward reform, the two fastest reformers—Kazakhstan and the Kyrgyz Republic—were at opposite ends of the spectrum, in many respects, at the outset of transformation, with Kazakhstan having a much richer resource base and a more diversified economic structure. These differences appear to have motivated each country to move in the same direction, by either taking quick advantage of initial relative strengths (as in Kazakhstan) or by striving to overcome initial limitations (as in the Kyrgyz Republic). By contrast, economic reforms in Turkmenistan and Uzbekistan—which fall somewhere in the middle along the spectrum of resource endowments and output diversity—were, for the most part, more sporadic and came in reaction to events rather than in anticipation of them. In Tajikistan, reform efforts were, until recently, constrained by civil conflict.

The initial years of transition were characterized by sharp output declines and an erosion in living standards in all the Central Asian states. In addition to severe disruptions to input supplies and traditional lines of production, special circumstances such as civil unrest in Tajikistan and an excessive reliance on traditional trade routes—particularly regional energy pipelines—in Kazakhstan and Turkmenistan constrained export markets and adversely affected growth. The negative impact on growth from structural dislocations was further aggravated by high inflation resulting from price liberalization and the monetization of large fiscal deficits to sustain output and employment, notably following the introduction of national currencies. By converse relationship, however, the speed with which inflation was reduced and the depth of structural reforms implemented were instrumental in the recoveries that were initiated during 1996–98. There is evidence in the region that steadfast implementation of stabilization policies

Table 1.1. Transition Economies: Selected Indicators, 1997[1]

	Population (in millions)	Per capita GDP[2] (in U.S. dollars)	Private sector (share in GDP)	Foreign trade (in percent of GDP)	FDI per capita (in U.S. dollars)	Asset share of state-owned banks	Average of EBRD transition indicators (1998)[3]
Central Asian states	**54.7**	**596**	**41**	**43**	**27**	**49**	**2+**
Kazakhstan	15.7	1,434	55[4]	31	84	45	3–
Kyrgyz Republic	4.6	366	60	38	18	10	3–
Tajikistan	6.1	179	20	69	2	...	2–
Turkmenistan	4.7	390	25	48	23	68	1+
Uzbekistan	23.6	611	45	26	7	71	2
Russia	**147.2**	**3,056**	**70**	**18**	**25**	**29**	**3–**
Other CIS	**82.1**	**746**	**43**	**32**	**45**	**28**	**2+**
Armenia	3.7	435	55	32	14	3	3–
Azerbaijan	7.6	509	40	28	144	81	2+
Belarus	10.2	1,314	20	60	19	55	2–
Georgia	5.4	968	55	14	35	0	3–
Moldova	4.3	504	45	24	15	0	3–
Ukraine	50.9	976	50	35	12	...	2+
Baltics	**7.7**	**2,674**	**67**	**51**	**69**	**19**	**3**
Estonia	1.5	3,230	70	61	8	0	3+
Latvia	2.5	2,211	60	41	139	7	3
Lithuania	3.7	2,581	70	50	59	49	3
Central and Eastern Europe	**111.3**	**3,516**	**62**	**38**	**76**	**44**	**3+**

Source: Data compiled from European Bank for Reconstruction and Development, Transition Report 1998.

[1] Other than for population, the group entries represent unweighted averages for the countries in the groups shown.

[2] EBRD estimates based on conversion of GDP in domestic currency to U.S. dollars using average 1997 exchange rates. The figures should be viewed as broadly indicative only, given the existence of multiple exchange rates and the associated conversion difficulties in some of the countries shown.

[3] EBRD transition indicators covering enterprise reform, financial sector reform, legal reform, and market and trade reform. Individual indicators range from 1 to 4+, with 4+ indicating the most progress in reforms (e.g., a 2– indicates more progress than 1+ but less progress than 2).

[4] According to IMF information, private sector share may be closer to 70 percent.

in the faster reformers produced, with expected lags, a positive output and investment response by boosting confidence in the economies and strengthening the perceptions of the newly emerging private sectors as to the consistency and sustainability of policies.

Success with stabilization, in addition to augmenting domestic savings, helped attract foreign direct investment (Kazakhstan), which aided the recovery process and brought in much needed capital and technological expertise. Improvements in factor efficiency associated with the reallocation of resources played an important role in the resumption of growth in some cases (Kazakhstan and the Kyrgyz Republic), but was less apparent in others (Turkmenistan and Uzbekistan). Trade liberalization also contributed to growth in the Central Asian states, at first by reinstating steady input supplies and, over time, by improving the efficiency of resource allocation, helping diversification, and ensuring greater transparency in the trade system.

While all the Central Asian countries suffered employment and real income losses during transition, unemployment lagged far behind sharp declines in output. The substantial real wage erosions experienced were partly compensated for by generous consumer subsidies and income from informal market activity, which are not adequately captured in the official statistics. Developments in employment and wages were also influenced by the degree to which countries were willing to restructure their state enterprise sectors. This entailed the imposition of hard budget constraints, notably the phasing out of budgetary support and directed credits to enterprises. In Turkmenistan, Tajikistan, and Uzbekistan, where such restructuring was delayed, open unemployment rates remained correspondingly low, notwithstanding persistent output contractions. Restructuring delays often reflected inadequacies in the social safety net systems to cope with the associated short-term disruptions to employment. Widespread disguised unemployment provided some protection, but at the expense of preventing reallocation of labor to more productive activities.

Given the loss of traditional revenue sources (particularly transfers from the Soviet budget) at the start of transition, the lack of domestic financing from nonbank sources, and limited access to international capital markets, the Central Asian states were left with little choice but to implement major fiscal structural reforms to meet their stabilization objectives in a sustainable fashion. Moreover, many of the reform measures—including price liberalization and exchange rate devaluation—tended to aggravate the fiscal deficits by raising expenditure more than revenue. While all the countries in the region underwent fiscal adjustment during the period reviewed, reductions in fiscal imbalances were accomplished pri-

marily by stop-gap measures. There was heavy reliance on expenditure sequestration and ad hoc revenue measures—particularly in the initial years of transition—and insufficient attention paid to growing payments arrears by governments and state enterprises. Moreover, large quasi-fiscal operations—conducted outside the budget, mainly by the banking sectors—weakened fiscal transparency and management. The adjustments that took place, therefore, represented only the first phase of a more substantive fiscal reform process, aimed at substantially rebuilding revenue and reprioritizing expenditure.

The Central Asian states, following the introduction of their national currencies, intensified efforts to stabilize their economies and sharply reduce inflation from peak rates of as high as four-digit levels. The countries were faced with a choice between adopting exchange rate or money-based stabilization programs. The two main arguments for an exchange rate peg—the instability of money demand during the turbulent transition period and the likelihood of the exchange rate overshooting with money-based stabilization—held sway in the Central Asian countries at the outset of transition. However, the conditions required to make this approach a success (notably restrained fiscal policies and ample international reserves) were mostly absent. Moreover, real shocks, such as sharp terms-of-trade shocks, could not effectively be absorbed if an exchange rate peg was chosen. All five countries, therefore, initially opted for money-based stabilization programs, with some exchange rate flexibility allowed under managed floats. Under these programs, the burden of stabilization fell primarily on fiscal adjustment, which entailed cuts in expenditure (notably real wages, subsidies, and capital outlays) and the tightening of budget constraints on state enterprises. Progress in the latter area varied across countries. Kazakhstan and the Kyrgyz Republic focused attention on state enterprise restructuring early on and eliminated directed credits, while the other countries in the group moved much more slowly.

Despite the absence of an exchange rate peg until mid-1998, considerable disinflation was achieved in all five countries, exchange rates were stabilized or even appreciated in real terms in some cases, and parallel market premiums were reduced (with the exception of Uzbekistan and, to a lesser extent, Turkmenistan). These moves were accompanied by a liberalization of exchange regimes at varied paces, again, with the faster reformers taking the lead. As stabilization took hold, Kazakhstan was confronted with having to protect its economy from destabilizing effects of surges in capital inflows. Protection entailed striking an appropriate balance between further fiscal tightening, sterilized interventions, and exchange rate appreciation. Most countries in the region, however, have not yet faced such tough policy challenges.

The financial crisis in Russia in August 1998 considerably altered the external economic environment for the Central Asian states. The crisis had an adverse economic impact on most of these countries, mainly because of declining Russian demand for their exports. Capital flows were also affected as foreign investors reassessed the risks of financing countries in the region and exchange rates came under heavy pressure. These developments brought to the fore the need to improve external debt management, following a period of sizable accumulated foreign liabilities by the countries, mainly to finance investment at a time of low domestic savings. Also, in countering the impact of the Russian crisis, the Central Asian states were faced with the challenge of resisting the temptation to reverse the exchange and trade liberalization policies already under way. Turkmenistan and Uzbekistan were less successful in meeting this challenge and intensified exchange controls. Other countries combined restrained financial policies with intervention in the exchange market to ward off the pressures on their economies in the aftermath of the Russian crisis.

Progress with structural reforms was mixed among the Central Asian states. All of the countries were relatively quick to initiate price liberalization, although their subsequent paces varied and there were instances of temporary reversals, primarily to guard against social unrest. In almost all instances, controlled prices were maintained for essential foodstuffs, energy, public transportation, and utilities. State enterprise restructuring proved particularly difficult, given the magnitude of the task and the reluctance of the authorities to face disruptions to production and the provision of social services by enterprises. Considerable progress was made in Kazakhstan and the Kyrgyz Republic, though, in initiating restructuring programs and in building the needed institutional frameworks. All countries experienced large domestic payments arrears in their state enterprise sectors, which partly mirrored the phasing out of the traditional sources of finance, such as directed credits, to this still dominant sector.

Privatization also proved to be a daunting task, although the faster reformers progressed considerably beyond the first stage of small enterprise privatization to mass privatization of medium- and large-scale enterprises. Encouraging progress was also made in initiating the privatization of agriculture through land-lease programs and the phasing out of state orders, although privatization of agricultural services fell behind. Legal and regulatory reforms, on the other hand, proceeded in piecemeal fashion, with only Kazakhstan and, more notably, the Kyrgyz Republic undertaking more in-depth re-

forms of their civil codes. All five countries passed bankruptcy laws at the outset of transition to liquidate persistently loss-making enterprises, although these laws were not rigorously implemented. They also enacted a series of laws to level the playing field for small and large enterprises and to promote competition. Nevertheless, much remains to be accomplished in these countries to achieve a simple and transparent regulatory framework that is fairly enforced.

Recently, the Central Asian states have focused increasingly on reforming their financial systems (both bank and nonbank) as an integral part of their stabilization and reform programs. Banks have not yet been transformed fully from administrators of financial flows to effective intermediaries between savers and investors, so that, again, more progress needs to be made in this area in the next stage of reforms. Also, nonbank financial systems need to be captured in adjustment operations, as is increasingly becoming the case in the Kyrgyz Republic.

Notwithstanding the progress to date, a heavy structural reform agenda remains for the Central Asian states, in order to strengthen their recent stabilization gains and to ensure sustainable and widely shared growth. Deeper and more persistent changes will be needed to improve the quality of fiscal adjustment; rehabilitate or liquidate state enterprises; strengthen banking systems and financial intermediation; restructure pension, health, and education systems; provide more affordable and well-targeted social safety nets; and broaden agricultural and other sectoral reforms. Finally, the scaling back of the still dominant public sectors and the firm integration of these economies into a market framework will require further progress in privatization, as well as continued modification of the extensive regulatory controls already in place. There will also be a growing need to strengthen legal and institutional reforms, as well as to address transparency and governance issues, with a view to limiting opportunities for corruption, enhancing public accountability, and promoting constructive links between governments and newly emerging private businesses.

This paper discusses the broad parameters of the prereform setting in the Central Asian states, including demographic features and natural resource endowments, and their possible impact on the approaches to reform. The paper also reviews the growth experiences of the Central Asian states during transition and finds that, apart from the predictable disruptions associated with transition and special factors such as civil strife, growth performance was influenced by success in achieving economic stabilization as well as by the scope and pace of structural reforms. Fiscal adjustment policies and the role of the public sector are examined, underscoring the desirability of further curtailing state involvement in these economies and of strengthening the quality of fiscal reforms. The experiences of the Central Asian states are also traced with regard to monetary policy reforms and stabilization since the introduction of their national currencies, focusing on the choice between monetary and exchange rate-based stabilization programs. Two sections examine external-sector reforms—including trade liberalization, market diversification, and currency reforms—and capital flows to the region, both in the form of foreign direct investment and official or private financing. Section VIII revisits and expands upon some of the areas covered in preceding sections, concentrating on the structural elements of reform to complement and strengthen the stabilization and growth efforts already under way. The paper concludes with key lessons to be drawn from the reform experiences of the Central Asian states and challenges for the future.

II   Prereform Setting and Conditions

Ivailo Izvorski

The five former states of Soviet Central Asia—Kazakhstan, the Kyrgyz Republic, Tajikistan, Turkmenistan, and Uzbekistan—extend from the Caspian Sea in the west to China in the east, and from central Siberia in the north to Afghanistan and the Islamic Republic of Iran in the south, covering a combined area equivalent to just over one-fifth of Russia's total land area. The region is rich in natural, agricultural, mineral, and fuel resources. Since the beginning of the 1990s, all five countries in the region have worked toward exploiting their resources more fully while moving their economies toward a market framework. Their progress with economic reforms has been influenced to a considerable extent by their political structures, ethnic characteristics, and remoteness from major world markets.

Political Environment

The five Central Asia states became independent in 1991, after more than a century of Russian and Soviet rule. Declarations of independence by these countries were backed by national referendums with overwhelming approval. In the presidential elections that followed, candidates mostly ran unopposed and won by sizable voting majorities. Subsequently, popular referendums extended the terms in office of presidents in Kazakhstan, Turkmenistan, and Uzbekistan and increased the authority of the president, relative to the legislature, in the Kyrgyz Republic. The Central Asian states adopted constitutions that lay a foundation for a parliamentary democracy but had mixed success with the promotion of individual rights and freedoms.

Following independence, the Central Asian states continued to maintain close ties with other countries in the region. They also became members of a number of multilateral organizations, including the IMF, the World Bank, the EBRD, and the Asian Development Bank. Kazakhstan and Uzbekistan currently hold observer status in the World Trade Organization and have applied to join; the Kyrgyz Republic joined the organization in October 1998. Turkmenistan officially adopted neutrality status, which was recognized by the United Nations in late 1995. Despite the predomi-

nance of Islam in these territories, the Central Asian states have tended to be cautious in their approach to neighboring Muslim countries, possibly for fear of alienating Russia,[1] or as a reflection of a reluctance to being closely identified with religious regimes. Among the Arab countries, Saudi Arabia has helped to develop religious infrastructures, such as schools, mosques, and religious centers, in these countries. Turkey has intensified political, cultural, and economic ties with the Central Asian states, and has emerged as a possible alternative to Russia as a transit way for oil and gas exports to European markets.

Demographic Characteristics

The Central Asian states display a mixed ethnic composition. Prior to independence, Russians accounted for a sizable proportion of the populations in Kazakhstan (38 percent) and the Kyrgyz Republic (22 percent), but constituted only 10 percent or less of the populations of Tajikistan, Turkmenistan, and Uzbekistan (Table 2.1). Ethnic Uzbeks were the second largest group in Tajikistan (24 percent) and constituted a significant proportion of the population in the Kyrgyz Republic (13 percent). In the region as a whole, Uzbeks were, by far, the largest ethnic group, followed by Russians and Kazakhs, with Kyrgyz and Turkmen being the smallest groups.

Ethnic tensions seriously threatened some of the Central Asian states. In Tajikistan,[2] political turmoil and civil strife escalated into a civil conflict in 1992, with devastating consequences. The conflict subsided in 1994 but violence sparked anew in 1996. Currently, peace is maintained under an agreement signed in mid-1997. Other tensions exist between ethnic groups within national borders, such as between the ethnic Kyrgyz and the ethnic Uzbek in the Kyrgyz Republic, as well as between separate states, such as Uzbekistan and Turkmenistan. Tensions and growing nationalism have led to the emigration of the Russians (employed

---

[1]See Hunter (1996).

[2]Tajikistan was part of the Uzbek Soviet Socialist Republic during 1925–29.

Table 2.1. Social and Demographic Indicators[1]

	Kazakhstan	Kyrgyz Republic	Tajikistan	Turkmenistan	Uzbekistan
Population (in millions)	15.7	4.7	5.9	4.7	23.7
Life expectancy at birth (in years)	68.0	67.0	68.0	65.0	68.0
Urban population (in percent of total)	58.0	38.0	32.0	45.0	41.0
Population growth (in percent)	−4.9[2]	1.3	1.5	2.5	1.9
Ethnic groups, 1990 (in percent)					
Kazakh	40	—	—	2	4
Kyrgyz	—	52	—	—	—
Russian	38	22	8	10	8
Tajik	—	—	63	—	5
Turkmen	—	—	—	73	—
Ukrainian	5	3	—	—	—
Uzbek	2	13	24	9	71
Other	15[3]	10[3]	5	6	12

Sources: National authorities; Pomfret (1995); Hunter (1996); and IMF Staff Country Reports.
[1]Unless otherwise noted, the indicators shown are for 1997 (for 1996 in the case of Tajikistan).
[2]The decline is explained by emigration, mostly of the Russian population.
[3]About 6 percent of Kazakhstan's population and 2 percent of the Kyrgyz Republic's population were German.

mostly in strategic industrial enterprises), thereby weakening human capital in these countries, but also easing the burden on social programs.

Resource Endowments and Initial Economic Structures

Agriculture plays an important role in the Central Asian states and provides employment for large segments of the populations. Soviet rule imposed a cotton monoculture on Turkmenistan, Uzbekistan, and Tajikistan and, to a lesser extent, on Kazakhstan and the Kyrgyz Republic. After the completion of the Karakum Canal in 1962, Turkmenistan became the second largest producer of cotton in the Soviet Union, and the tenth largest in the world, while Uzbekistan grew to be the world's third largest cotton exporter (about one-half of the country's export revenue came from cotton in 1992). The Kyrgyz Republic had a small cotton sector, given its mountainous territory. Kazakhstan's agricultural sector was more diversified. Not only did it become self-sufficient in grain production, but Kazakhstan also became a net grain exporter in the region (though yields were much lower than in the two major grain producers, Russia and Ukraine). Kazakhstan, moreover, developed a strong industrial sector and was the only country in the region where agricultural employment was below industrial employment.

A number of the Central Asian states are endowed with rich energy resources—natural gas, oil, coal, and hydro energy. Kazakhstan, the only Central Asian net exporter of oil, had 85 percent of the region's proven oil reserves and was the second largest oil producer in the Soviet Union after Russia.[3] Kazakhstan also provided one-fifth of the Soviet Union's coal, most of it used in electricity generation and in the processing of iron. Turkmenistan had almost one-half of the proven gas reserves of the Central Asian region and became the fourth largest gas exporter in the world at the beginning of the 1990s when gas exports exceeded 80 billion cubic meters. Uzbekistan was the only other net gas exporter in the region. Currently, the greatest oil reserves potential is around the Caspian Sea, an area contested by the littoral states. While the Kyrgyz Republic and Tajikistan do not have significant gas and oil deposits, the abundant hydro resources of the Amu Darya and Syr Darya Rivers have turned these countries into major producers of hydroelectricity. Energy resources were redistributed within the Union of Soviet Socialist Republics (U.S.S.R.) and sold to international customers through a regional network of oil and gas pipelines. Following independence, the Central Asian states continued to rely on these pipelines, which remained under Russian control, for trade in energy products.

[3]See World Bank (1993).

Table 2.2. Selected Economic Indicators Prior to Transition
(In percent)

	Kazakhstan	Kyrgyz Republic	Tajikistan	Turkmenistan	Uzbekistan
Origin of GDP, 1990					
Industry	21	26	29	16	24
Agriculture	42	32	38	48	44
Construction	16	8	15	18	15
Net Material Product (NMP) growth rates					
1971–85	3.1	4.2	4.4	3.1	5.1
1986–89	1.9	4.9	3.2	4.9	2.9
NMP per capita growth rates (averages)					
1971–85	1.8	2.1	1.4	0.4	2.2
1986–89	0.9	2.9	0.0	2.2	0.3
Share of private sector output in GDP, 1990[1]	7.0	7.3	1.0	9.9	10.0
Total trade as percent of NMP, 1988	33.9	45.2	41.6	39.3	39.5
Intraregional trade as share of total, 1988[2]	86.3	86.9	86.3	89.1	85.8
Exports to CMEA as percent of NMP, 1990	18.0	21.0	22.0	34.0	24.0

Sources: Pomfret (1995); IMF and others (1991); Spencer and Ross (1992); EBRD (1996); and EBRD (1997).
[1]Private sector as defined in the EBRD *Transition Reports*.
[2]Within the former Soviet Union.

In addition to energy resources, the Central Asian states have abundant deposits of gold, iron ore, and other minerals. One-third of the gold in the former Soviet Union was produced in the Kyzylkum Desert, making Uzbekistan the second largest gold producer in the Soviet Union and the eighth largest in the world. About one-half of the Soviet Union's silver, and one-fifth of its gold, was produced in Kazakhstan. The Kyrgyz Republic's Kumtor gold mine is the eighth largest in the world.

Despite rich natural resource endowments and the potential for industrial development, the Central Asian states, with the exception of Kazakhstan, were biased toward production and export of raw materials and cotton-based agriculture. The share of agriculture far exceeded the share of industry in these countries' GDP (Table 2.2). Agricultural wages were typically much lower than industrial wages in the Soviet Union, and agricultural wages in Central Asia were less than one-half of comparable wages elsewhere in the Soviet Union.[4] The Central Asian states, therefore, had much lower per capita incomes relative to the rest of the U.S.S.R.

Bibliography

Blanchard, Olivier, 1997, *The Economics of Post-Communist Transition* (New York: Oxford University Press).

Bruno, Michael, 1993, "Stabilization and the Macroeconomics of Transition—How Different is Eastern Europe?" *Economics of Transition*, Vol. 1 (January 1993), pp. 5–19.

European Bank for Reconstruction and Development, 1996, *Transition Report* (London: EBRD).

———, 1997, *Transition Report* (London: EBRD).

Hunter, Shireen T., 1996, *Central Asia Since Independence*, The Washington Papers No. 168 (Washington: The Center for Strategic and International Studies; Westport: Praeger Publishers).

International Monetary Fund, World Bank, Organization for Economic Cooperation and Development, European Bank for Reconstruction and Development, 1991, *A Study of the Soviet Economy*, Vol. 1 (Washington: International Monetary Fund).

Library of Congress, Federal Research Division, 1997, *Kazakhstan, Kyrgyzstan, Tajikistan, Turkmenistan, and Uzbekistan: Country Studies*, ed. by Glenn E. Curtis, Area Handbook Series (Washington: U.S. Government Printing Office).

Pomfret, Richard W.T., 1995, *The Economies of Central Asia* (Princeton: Princeton University Press).

Rashid, Ahmed, 1994, *The Resurgence of Central Asia: Islam or Nationalism?* (Karachi, Pakistan: Oxford University Press; London: Zed Books).

Spencer, Grant H., and Paul S. Ross, 1992, *Common Issues and Interrepublic Relations in the Former U.S.S.R.*, IMF Economic Review (Washington: International Monetary Fund).

World Bank, 1993, *Kazakhstan: The Transition to a Market Economy*, World Bank Country Study (Washington).

[4]International Monetary Fund and others (1991).

III   Growth, Employment, and Real Incomes

Ivailo Izvorski and Emine Gürgen

The differences in resource endowments and initial economic conditions influenced attitudes toward economic transformation in the Central Asian states. In 1992, Saparmurat Niyazov campaigned for the presidency of Turkmenistan on the platform that the country's rich gas and oil resources would turn it into the Kuwait of Central Asia. Economic reforms were postponed largely on the expectation that sharp initial gains in the terms of trade and subsequent opening up of new export markets for the country's energy resources would allow for a gradual pace of reform. Likewise, Uzbekistan's preindependence specialization in cotton and gold, and its self-sufficiency in energy, may have contributed to its reliance on a more gradual and state-led approach to economic transformation.[1] While cotton and gold exports were successfully redirected to new markets, a fall in the world price of gold forced the authorities to rethink their strategy and to introduce a comprehensive reform package in 1994, which became stalled by 1996. By contrast, Kazakhstan, the third most resource-rich state in Central Asia, refrained from overreliance on a single product (oil) and pursued a more decisive approach to transformation. In addition, its close economic ties to Russia and a significant Russian population within its territory made it advantageous for Kazakhstan to reform at a comparable and, in some areas, at an even faster rate than Russia, in order to minimize the disruptions to economic relations between the two countries.

Apart from differences in initial conditions, the economic transformation and growth experiences of the Central Asian states reflected divergences between states that started economic reforms early and pursued bold adjustment programs (Kazakhstan and the Kyrgyz Republic) and states that were late reformers and less consistent in their adjustment efforts (Uzbekistan, Turkmenistan, and Tajikistan). Success in bringing inflation under control, coupled with the early introduction of systemic changes, played an important role in promoting economic re-

coveries. In addition to the predictable disruptions to input supplies and production associated with the initial phase of transition, there were some special factors involved, such as civil conflict in Tajikistan and strong reliances on preindependence trade routes (notably by Kazakhstan and Turkmenistan on the Russian-controlled regional energy pipelines), which constrained exports and adversely affected growth performance.

Growth Experience of the Central Asian States

The years following independence were characterized by a sharp deterioration in growth performance in all five Central Asian states (Table 3.1 and Figure 3.1). During 1992–96, real GDP declined—on average, by 37 percent cumulatively in these countries—somewhat less than the average 44 percent for the Commonwealth of Independent States (CIS). There was considerable variation across countries, however, with the cumulative drop in real GDP ranging from 16 percent in Uzbekistan to almost 60 percent in Tajikistan. By 1996, Kazakhstan, the Kyrgyz Republic, and Uzbekistan achieved positive growth, followed by Tajikistan in 1997 and Turkmenistan in 1998. These last two countries had started their recovery from very low levels of output. The recovery process suffered a setback in the aftermath of the financial turmoil in Russia in August 1998. The magnitude of the external shock led to a noticeable slowdown in economic activity throughout the region, particularly in Kazakhstan and the Kyrgyz Republic, as exports to Russia and other affected countries fell.

Growth Performance and Underlying Factors

Recent empirical studies[2] indicate that the speed at which inflation is reduced and the pace and depth of structural reforms are important influences on the

---

[1]See Zettelmeyer (1998) on the Uzbek growth experience.

[2]See Havrylyshyn and others (1998).

Table 3.1. Growth and Inflation
(In percent)

	1992	1993	1994	1995	1996	1997	1998 Prov.
Real GDP Growth							
Kazakhstan	−5.3	−9.2	−12.6	−8.2	0.5	1.7	−2.5
Kyrgyz Republic	−13.9	−15.5	−20.1	−5.4	7.1	9.9	2.0
Tajikistan	−29.0	−11.0	−21.5	−12.5	−4.4	1.7	5.3
Turkmenistan	−5.3	−10.2	−19.0	−8.2	−7.7	−25.9	4.8
Uzbekistan	−11.0	−2.3	−4.2	−0.9	1.6	2.4	2.8
Average CIS	−21.2	−11.9	−15.1	−5.4	−0.3	1.6	2.1
Inflation (end-of-period)							
Kazakhstan	2,962.8	2,169.1	1,160.3	60.4	28.6	11.3	1.9
Kyrgyz Republic	1,257.0	766.9	95.7	32.3	34.9	14.7	18.4
Tajikistan	...	7,343.7	1.1	2,135.2	40.5	163.6	2.7
Turkmenistan	644.0	1,400.0	1,328.5	1,261.5	445.9	21.4	19.8
Uzbekistan	910.0	884.8	1,281.4	116.9	64.4	50.2	26.1
Average CIS	1,627.2	3,838.8	1,390.8	363.4	63.0	32.2	24.9

Sources: National authorities; and IMF staff estimates.

growth performance of transition economies. During the initial years of transition (1990–93), output decline was minimized in those countries that either implemented substantial reforms or attempted to

Figure 3.1. Developments in Real GDP
(Index, 1991 = 100)

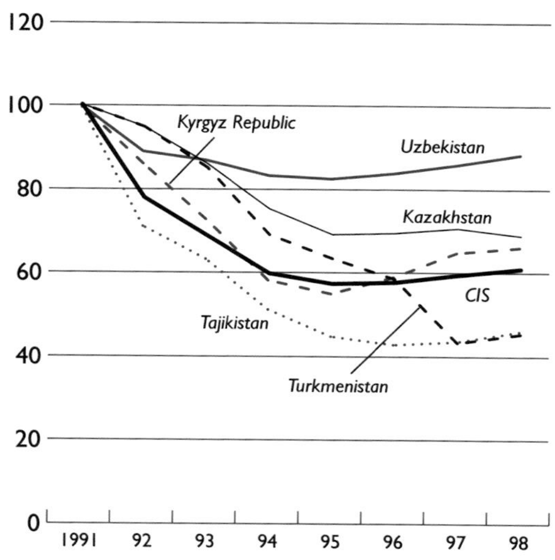

Sources: National authorities; and IMF staff estimates.

preserve the status quo, while intermediate reformers suffered sharp output declines. In the later years of transition (1994–98), bold reform efforts taken in the earlier period paid off and growth strengthened. Unlike the asymmetric effect of structural reforms, bringing inflation under control was beneficial for growth throughout the transition.

By way of illustrating the importance of stabilization and structural reforms on growth in the Central Asian states, Figure 3.2 plots the average real GDP growth rates for 1990–98 against average inflation (top panel) and an average reform index[3] (bottom panel) for 25 transition economies in Central and Eastern Europe, and for Russia, the Baltics, and other countries of the former Soviet Union (BRO countries). The straight lines represent simple ordinary least squares regression fits. While the exercise should be regarded as no more than indicative, given the data deficiencies and the usual difficulties associated with cross-country comparisons, some broad conclusions can be drawn. The bottom panel of Figure 3.2 illustrates that growth in Kazakhstan, the Kyrgyz Republic, and Tajikistan have been approximately in line with the prediction regarding the impact of structural reforms on growth. Uzbekistan and, to a lesser extent, Turkmenistan appear not to follow this pattern, indicating a weaker link between their reform efforts and growth performance. In the top panel, the implications of inflation performance for growth are similar. For all the countries, except

[3]Derived from the EBRD transition indicators.

Figure 3.2. Impact of Inflation and Reform on Growth

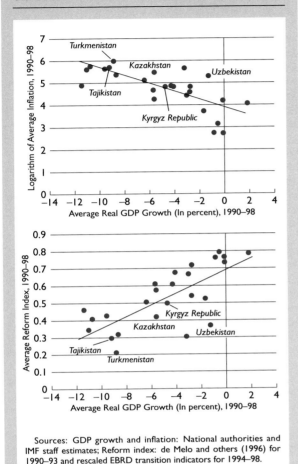

Sources: GDP growth and inflation: National authorities and IMF staff estimates; Reform index: de Melo and others (1996) for 1990–93 and rescaled EBRD transition indicators for 1994–98.

with trade liberalization—influenced growth in the Central Asian states.

In Kazakhstan, following a cumulative decline in real GDP of more than 30 percent during 1992–95, modest growth was recorded during 1996–97, but output fell by 2.5 percent in 1998 owing to the impact of the Russian crisis. Apart from macroeconomic instability, limited transport capacity for oil exports and serious inefficiencies in the state enterprise sector contributed to the earlier adverse growth performance. In the Kyrgyz Republic, after a cumulative contraction of 45 percent during 1992–95, growth averaged about 8 percent annually during 1996–97 and dropped to 2 percent in 1998. The initial poor growth performance was associated with the failure to reallocate resources to sectors with comparative advantage due to structural rigidities. Subsequent recovery reflected success in overcoming such problems, with the agricultural and gold mining sectors emerging as the key contributors to growth. By contrast, Uzbekistan's growth performance was disrupted less at the outset of independence. Real GDP declined cumulatively by only 17 percent during 1992–95, with a modest but progressive recovery during 1996–98. A recent study[4] indicates that the less pronounced transitional recession experienced by Uzbekistan, despite the inadequacies in macroeconomic and structural policies, may have been attributable partly to favorable initial conditions, notably a low level of industrialization and a dominant cotton sector. At the same time, Uzbekistan was not dependent on energy imports and did not have to rely on energy exports to nonpaying regional markets. Industrial production could, therefore, be sustained through cheap energy supplies and subsidies financed partly by agricultural exports.

Economic recovery in Tajikistan was delayed by a civil conflict that persisted from shortly after independence in 1991 until the signing of a peace agreement in mid-1997. The cumulative drop in real GDP nearly reached 60 percent during 1992–96, before recovery started in 1997 following peace and the start of a comprehensive reform program. In Turkmenistan—where growth performance was heavily influenced by developments in access to export markets for natural gas and its trading partners' reduced ability to make payments—real GDP declined each year during 1992–97, resulting in a cumulative contraction of nearly 60 percent in this period. The largest single drop (26 percent) occurred in 1997 when gas exports were discontinued in response to deteriorating payments. Inefficiencies in the agricul-

Uzbekistan, the relationship between growth performance and inflation is close to what was predicted; Uzbekistan displays higher growth rates than would be supported by its progress with stabilization. The discrepancies for Uzbekistan may be explained by the momentum arising from the favorable initial conditions noted earlier, while overall growth performance in Turkmenistan during the period appears to have been influenced predominantly by the wide annual swings in gas exports associated with the access to pipelines and the payments difficulties of trading partners.

Outside of this broader framework, some evidence suggests that specific variables—such as success in reallocating resources to sectors with comparative advantage, the ability to sustain domestic investment and attract foreign investment, improvements in factor productivity, and progress

---

[4]See Taube and Zettelmeyer (1998).

tural sector also contributed to the adverse growth performance. Growth finally resumed in 1998, although from very low output levels, reflecting favorable harvests and buoyant oil production, which were partly in response to increased investments in these sectors.

Investment declined sharply in the early years of transformation in all five Central Asian states, but rebounded subsequently in most of them, although not always fully to earlier levels. In Kazakhstan, the investment ratio declined from about 26 percent during 1991–93 to 12 percent in 1996, and recovered to 15 percent in 1997. Investment by the state sector suffered the largest cutbacks, while investment by the nonstate sector held steady in real terms, and even rose in transportation, communication, and industry (with a major reallocation in industry toward oil and gas extraction activities and nonferrous metallurgy). In Uzbekistan, the investment ratio fell sharply during 1992–94, but rebounded in 1995–97 on the strength of government-led investment in priority sectors with foreign financing (oil refineries) or joint ventures with foreign investors (electronics, gold mining, and telecommunications). The government also invested heavily in hotel construction and the restoration of tourism sites, although there was very little investment in agriculture, despite its importance to the economy. In the Kyrgyz Republic, the investment ratio fell steadily during the first few years of transition, from about 20 percent of GDP in 1992 to 9 percent in 1994, but then almost doubled in 1996, mostly reflecting construction activity related to the Kumtor gold mine. Investment in Tajikistan collapsed after independence, mainly because of the civil conflict. In contrast to other Central Asian states, Turkmenistan's investment ratio appears not to have decreased much following independence, reflecting heavy government investment (partly foreign-financed) in major infrastructure projects with low returns (such as hotels, monuments, palaces, airports, and aircraft), but also investment in the oil and gas sector. Ongoing sizable foreign investment in a major oil refinery is expected to further boost output and exports of oil products in the near future.

The reform process in Kazakhstan was aided by significant foreign direct investment (FDI) during 1992–98, mainly in the energy and metallurgical industries (see Section VII). This reflected the establishment of a framework for FDI early in the transition period, the implementation of an ambitious privatization program, and an attempt to bring in foreign management and technological expertise through management contracts. By contrast, Uzbekistan attracted relatively little FDI, mainly for a few large projects, such as gold mining and car production. FDI flows, which rose from $9 million in 1992 to $100 million in 1995, dampened in 1996 in re-

sponse to restrictive foreign exchange and trade policies. In the Kyrgyz Republic, FDI strengthened during 1994–97 to a cumulative total of almost $280 million, mainly due to the Kumtor gold project. The shortage of mineral resources in the Kyrgyz Republic and long distances to developed markets, though, were major obstacles to FDI. Foreign investors also showed little interest in the country's privatization program. FDI flows into Turkmenistan remained well below levels the country is capable of attracting, given its rich resource base, because of limited markets for its energy exports and an unstable economic environment. Nevertheless, cumulative FDI reached over $600 million during 1994–98, reflecting foreign investment in the oil sector (aided by a new petroleum law) and, to a lesser extent, in the textile industry. With civil unrest and political and economic instability, FDI in Tajikistan has been confined to modest investment in gold mines.

Improvements in factor efficiency appear to have contributed to output recovery in some Central Asian states. In Kazakhstan, increased efficiency associated with the reallocation of resources has played a significant role in the recent resumption of growth. Total factor productivity is estimated to have risen by 1.5 percent in 1996 and by 4 percent in 1997, following sharp declines in the preceding years. By contrast, in Uzbekistan, the reallocation of resources has been limited, reflecting the slow pace of structural reforms, and there do not appear to have been notable efficiency gains outside of the new service sector and joint ventures with foreign partners. There is some evidence that efficiency has not improved in state-owned agriculture, where yields per hectare and per livestock unit have either stagnated or fallen. In the Kyrgyz Republic, agriculture was the first sector to benefit from the reallocation of resources and contributed to the resumption of growth in 1996. The distribution of land-use rights to individual farmers early in the transition process improved incentives and attracted idle resources from other sectors. Although marginal efficiency in agriculture remained low by international standards, it was higher than in other sectors of the Kyrgyz economy, with the efficiency of private farms exceeding that of cooperative and state farms. Very little resource reallocation has taken place in Turkmenistan, given the general lack of reforms. Some improvements have occurred in agricultural yields (cotton and grain) following the provision of inputs, fertilizers, and financing to farmers under a land-lease program launched in late 1996. Finally, in Tajikistan, available data suggest a sharp decline in efficiency, with labor productivity plummeting in all sectors of the economy and agricultural yields falling, except in wheat production, which benefited from some early privatization.

Trade liberalization (see also Section VI) was another important factor influencing growth in the Central Asian states. Progress with trade liberalization contributed significantly to growth in Kazakhstan, as most new investment was in the import-intensive energy sector. Similarly, maintenance of a liberal trade regime (even after joining the customs union with Russia, Belarus, and Kazakhstan) greatly assisted the Kyrgyz Republic in promoting exports. Uzbekistan's import regime was partly liberalized in late 1995 and the first half of 1996, and access to foreign exchange was simultaneously eased. The resulting increase in imported consumer goods contributed significantly to the expansion of the service sector and to the overall recovery of the economy. A later tightening of exchange controls in response to emerging balance of payments pressures, however, reversed this trend. Likewise, in Turkmenistan, where there are no formal trade restrictions, foreign trade is essentially conducted by state enterprises under close government control and access to foreign exchange is limited to priority sectors. There has, therefore, been little impetus for growth through trade liberalization. There may also have been some hindrances from exchange controls, which triggered shortages of imported inputs and consumer goods. Trade liberalization in Tajikistan may have helped to slow the pace of economic decline in two distinct ways. First, the liberalization of grain imports helped develop a dynamic private sector to replace the inefficient state bread complex; liberalization combined with the initial land reform boosted domestic grain production. Second, foreign suppliers provided inputs to cotton farmers following the liberalization of cotton marketing, thereby strengthening cotton production and exports.

The Emerging Private Sector

There is clear evidence of emerging nonstate or private sector activity in the Central Asian states, although the extent of transformation varies considerably among countries. According to recent EBRD estimates (based on both official and unofficial sources), private sector shares in GDP ranged from 20 percent in Tajikistan to 60 percent in the Kyrgyz Republic in 1997, with percentage shares in Kazakhstan and Uzbekistan closer to the upper end of the range and Turkmenistan nearer the lower end. Estimates that only include companies with majority private ownership indicate much lower shares (e.g., 35 percent in Kazakhstan compared with 55 percent given by EBRD estimates). A great deal of uncertainty is also related to these estimates, because of the lack of reliable and comprehensive statistics on private sector activity, and possible differences in definitions. For example, in Turkmenistan, official data indicate an 18 percent private sector share com-

pared with 25 percent in EBRD estimates, and World Bank estimates put the private sector share at 10–15 percent. In Kazakhstan, there appears to be conflicting information on the share of the private sector. Nevertheless, the private sector is generally gaining importance in the Central Asian states, particularly in those countries where reforms have firmly taken hold and where structural changes that are conducive to a favorable business environment are being implemented, such as in Kazakhstan and the Kyrgyz Republic.

Employment and Real Incomes

In the Central Asian states, sharp output declines during transition were not matched by growth in officially recorded unemployment, although data covering unemployment suffer from serious deficiencies. For example, unemployed persons who received benefits for more than six months are excluded from the statistics in Kazakhstan, and persons not actively seeking employment are not captured in the official unemployment statistics in Turkmenistan. The official figures, moreover, do not account for disguised unemployment. Beyond statistical shortcomings, however, guaranteed state employment continues to constitute an integral part of the social safety net in these countries.[5] Labor hoarding is particularly severe in agriculture, where families work either on leased plots of land or in cooperatives. State-owned industrial enterprises also refrain from labor layoffs in times of output contraction. Therefore, only a very small portion of the economically active population is officially registered as unemployed. Even after allowing for data deficiencies and disguised unemployment, it seems unlikely, though, that the drop in employment in the Central Asian states during transition has been of similar orders of magnitude as their declines in real GDP.

With sharp declines in output following independence, and little or no open unemployment, real wages in the Central Asian states typically plummeted in the early years of transition (Table 3.2 and Figure 3.3). Real wages fluctuated considerably but began to recover after mid-1995, reflecting moderation in inflation as reform programs took hold. The exceptions were Turkmenistan, where the recovery came later, and Tajikistan, where real wages, after declining sharply through early 1996, recovered slightly and remained more or less flat because of the civil conflict and the associated delay in reforms. Measured in dollar terms, wages showed a similar

---

[5]In Turkmenistan and Tajikistan each citizen is still officially guaranteed employment.

Table 3.2. Real Wages[1]
(1993: QI = 100)

	Kazakhstan	Kyrgyz Republic	Tajikistan	Turkmenistan	Uzbekistan
1993: QI	100.0	100.0	100.0	100.0	100.0
QII	105.2	91.4	66.5	151.6	133.1
QIII	104.8	90.7	45.8	194.9	233.8
QIV	92.6	86.8	20.7	176.0	193.3
1994: QI	55.7	76.6	18.4	141.3	159.7
QII	69.1	76.0	20.3	78.6	105.4
QIII	67.4	77.3	17.6	81.3	115.0
QIV	72.5	87.2	18.0	49.0	119.4
1995: QI	64.8	79.8	12.9	55.0	92.4
QII	70.2	82.6	13.5	47.4	94.2
QIII	77.0	87.0	9.0	73.0	94.3
QIV	82.7	98.8	3.4	35.5	123.9
1996: QI	67.9	82.5	2.3	22.9	113.1
QII	71.2	79.3	2.0	28.8	123.7
QIII	73.8	85.4	3.7	32.0	140.6
QIV	77.0	91.4	4.6	45.8	154.3
1997: QI	71.6	77.5	4.7	48.2	129.5
QII	75.5	78.3	3.7	61.2	116.6
QIII	79.2	87.9	2.9	63.3	135.7
QIV	83.9	99.9	3.4	65.6	153.5
1998: QI	77.5	89.5	3.5	62.5	132.9
QII	80.2	92.9	3.8	78.8	133.6
QIII	82.7	99.8	4.9	82.6	163.4

Source: IMF staff estimates.
[1]Nominal wage index deflated by the consumer price index.

pattern. At the end of the third quarter of 1998, dollar wages were the highest in Kazakhstan ($127), followed by Uzbekistan ($58) and Turkmenistan ($54), the Kyrgyz Republic ($37), and lastly, Tajikistan ($12).

Average real and dollar wages, however, do not give a complete description of real incomes in the Central Asian states. Workers generally hold more than one job and often receive supplemental in-kind income and services such as housing and child care from their primary employers (up to 20 percent of the base wage in the Kyrgyz Republic). Government employees often have very generous leave allowances. Moreover, incomes continue to be augmented in all five Central Asian states by consumer subsidies on basic food staples as well as utilities and transportation. For example, in late 1997, direct food subsidies in Turkmenistan accounted for more than 15 percent of the average wage, while total consumer subsidies were estimated to be equivalent to the average wage. So far, only in Kazakhstan and the Kyrgyz Republic have price subsidies mostly been

eliminated (see Section VIII). State-provided education and medical care are still in place in these countries, although the quality has dropped significantly, and household incomes are often supplemented by one or more types of social benefits, including pensions. Generally, these benefits tend not to be well targeted, resulting in large groups of the population receiving relatively low benefits.

Finally, given the substantial size of the unofficial economy in these countries, it is likely that real incomes are much higher than real wages, even after adjustment for in-kind payments, consumer subsidies, and social benefits. For example, it has been estimated that the unofficial economy has produced goods and services equivalent to 34 percent of GDP in 1995 in Kazakhstan, and 7 percent of GDP in Uzbekistan.[6] Official estimates put the size of the informal sector in Turkmenistan at 12–18 percent of GDP.

---

[6]See Kaufmann and Kaliberda (1996).

Figure 3.3. Wage Developments

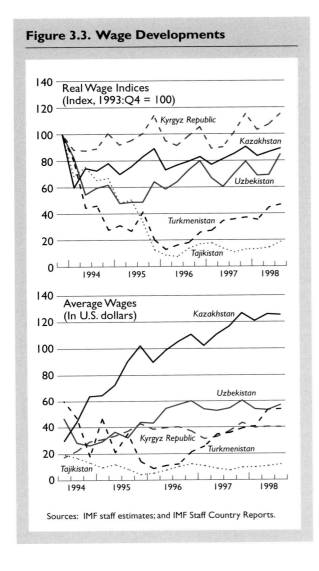

Sources: IMF staff estimates; and IMF Staff Country Reports.

Bibliography

Citrin, Daniel A., and Ashok K. Lahiri, eds., 1995, *Policy Experiences and Issues in the Baltics, Russia, and Other Countries of the Former Soviet Union*, IMF Occasional Paper No. 133 (Washington: International Monetary Fund).

de Melo, Martha, Cevdet Denizer, and Alan Gelb, 1996, "From Plan to Market: Patterns of Transition," World Bank Policy Research Working Paper No. 1564 (Washington: World Bank).

European Bank for Reconstruction and Development, 1996, *Transition Report* (London: EBRD).

_____, 1997, *Transition Report* (London: EBRD).

Fischer, Stanley, Ratna Sahay, and Carlos A. Végh, 1996, "Stabilization and Growth in Transition Economies: The Early Experience," IMF Working Paper 96/31 (Washington: International Monetary Fund).

Ghosh, Atish, and Steven Phillips, 1998, "Inflation, Disinflation, and Growth," IMF Working Paper 98/68 (Washington: International Monetary Fund).

Havrylyshyn, Oleh, Ivailo Izvorski, and Ron van Rooden, 1998, "Recovery and Growth in Transition Economies 1990–97: A Stylized Regression Analysis," IMF Working Paper 98/141 (Washington: International Monetary Fund).

Havrylyshyn, Oleh, Thomas Wolf, Julian Berengaut, Marta de Castello Branco, Ron van Rooden, and Valerie Mercer-Blackman, (forthcoming), *Growth Experience in Transition Countries 1990–98*, IMF Occasional Paper No. 184 (Washington: International Monetary Fund).

Hernándes-Catá, Ernesto, 1997, "Liberalization and the Behavior of Output During the Transition from Plan to Market," IMF Working Paper 97/53 (Washington: International Monetary Fund).

International Monetary Fund, 1995, "Disinflation, Growth, and Foreign Direct Investment in Transition Countries," in *World Economic Outlook, May 1995*, World Economic and Financial Surveys (Washington).

_____, 1996, "Long-Term Growth Potential in the Countries in Transition," in *World Economic Outlook, October 1996*, World Economic and Financial Surveys (Washington).

Kaufmann, Daniel, and Aleksander Kaliberda, 1996, "Integrating the Unofficial Economy into the Dynamics of Post-Socialist Economies: A Framework for Analysis and Evidence," World Bank Policy Research Working Paper No. 1691 (Washington: World Bank).

Taube, Günther, and Jeromin Zettelmeyer, 1998, "The Decline and Recovery in Uzbekistan: Past Performance and Future Prospects," IMF Working Paper 98/132 (Washington: International Monetary Fund).

Zettelmeyer, Jeromin, 1998, "The Uzbek Growth Puzzle," IMF Working Paper 98/133 (Washington: International Monetary Fund).

IV   Fiscal Adjustment

Jon Craig

The public sectors of the Central Asian states still exhibit many of the characteristics of the former Soviet Union. Although the measured size of the public sector, relative to GDP, has been reduced in all countries, governments continue to exert a strong influence on most aspects of economic activity through traditional budgetary operations (central and local budgets as well as various extrabudgetary funds); quasi-fiscal operations performed by the state-owned financial and nonfinancial enterprises; extensive regulation of several aspects of economic and social activity; and informal links enabling government administrators to influence and guide decisions by state enterprise managers and many seemingly privatized enterprises.[1] The relative size of the general government sector in these economies was curtailed by the persistent decline in the revenue base (see Section VIII), limited capacities of these countries to access foreign funding, and the need to contain fiscal deficits to levels compatible with restrained financial policies, rather than by discrete measures to contain government operations.

Role of the Public Sector

At the outset of the adjustment process, insufficient attention was paid to cutting back public sector responsibilities in the Central Asian states. As a result, most of the countries reviewed continue to retain formal responsibility for large public sectors (including quasi-fiscal operations outside of the budget, as noted before), not much smaller than what existed under the Soviet Union. In addition to the traditional functions of defense, foreign affairs, and law enforcement, most states maintain extensive public education and health systems and elaborate—although often poorly targeted—social security arrangements. Governments

also continue to bear responsibility for the bulk of the deteriorating infrastructures from the socialist period, including transport facilities, public utilities, and state property. Substantial involvement also continues in a number of areas less central to traditional public sector functions, including recreation and cultural activities, housing, scientific research, and regulation of economic services such as power supplies and transportation. Finally, there is extravagant state spending in some of the Central Asian states (notably Turkmenistan) on public buildings, monuments, and sports and cultural facilities.

Faced with financial constraints, however, governments have had to contain expenditure. For much of the period surveyed, expenditure restraint has largely relied on across-the-board measures, with the emphasis on compression via sequestration, wage and staff freezes, postponement of capital projects, and neglect of essential maintenance on existing facilities. There has been growing recognition in these countries that such an approach, if sustained, would substantially erode the overall quality of key services and infrastructure. Efforts have been stepped up to modify the role of the public sector. Actual recognition of the likely permanence of revenue constraints has encouraged the adoption of measures to cut spending and to promote private sector provision of selected services, particularly in health and education. In Kazakhstan, the local government sector is in the process of privatizing the operations of a number of health care, education, scientific, cultural, and sports facilities. The licensing of private education institutions has increased almost sixfold since 1995, though it started from a low base. Substantial progress has recently been made in streamlining social safety nets in the Central Asian states, with some countries taking steps to completely eliminate or substantially replace untargeted and costly budget subsidies with more cost-effective cash benefit payments. Several countries now have some privatized health sector activities such as pharmacies. Pension reform is also high on the agenda for most of these countries, notably Kazakhstan (see Section VIII).

---

[1]One example of informal influence is the frequent granting of preferential treatment (e.g., tax concessions) to enterprises in which the government continues to hold a direct interest, often in the form of a joint venture, which permits these enterprises to operate under less strict commercial structures.

Meanwhile, decreasing the public service role of state-owned enterprises has necessitated additional spending by local governments. In Kazakhstan and the Kyrgyz Republic, state enterprises have begun to divest social assets, such as preschools and health care facilities, to local governments, which have attempted to fund these activities with taxes and other revenues. Because the standards of services provided by local governments (with their limited resources) do not always match the standards of profitable enterprises, there remains some pressure for the state enterprise sector to retain these services. For example, in some towns in Turkmenistan, the state gas company retains responsibility for schools and other facilities, which local governments would have difficulty financing. The broader task of privatizing state enterprises (discussed in Section VIII), particularly the larger enterprises and those engaged in utilities, is also proving to be a slow and difficult task within the region, although Kazakhstan and the Kyrgyz Republic have made encouraging starts. Privatization of medium and large public enterprises has been a slower process in Uzbekistan, and it has barely begun in Tajikistan and Turkmenistan. The reasons are primarily because of ongoing civil strife and legal impediments in Tajikistan, and strong resistance by the line ministries and an overvaluation of the few enterprises that were put up for sale in Turkmenistan. In almost all of these countries, state enterprises are being commercialized as a first step toward their eventual sale.

Most Central Asian states continue to use their still largely government-controlled banking sectors to perform quasi-fiscal activities; deficits are often incurred by such operations. In Kazakhstan, for example, public debt guarantees and use of the banking system to clear public sector arrears were major factors contributing to the quasi-fiscal deficit in the period before 1995. In Turkmenistan, the cost of highly subsidized, directed credits—the government authorized lending through the central bank to sectors designated as being of national importance[2]—is essentially met by the seigniorage and other profits of the central bank that, in turn, reduces revenues from profit transfers to the budget. The cost of such activities is not presently shown as part of general government operations. There are also no provisions for government-guaranteed loans (some to finance the cotton sector, others to meet construction costs of government projects) in the budget,[3] although these loans partly finance quasi-fiscal activities and are often called in. Crop financing arrangements, similar to those in Turkmenistan, also exist in Uzbekistan, and on occasion, large on-lending allocations in the budget must be made to the agricultural sector to cover the servicing of outstanding farm debt. As in Turkmenistan, guarantees on foreign loans contracted for cotton financing and capital projects are not captured as quasi-fiscal activity of the public sector.

In addition to the more explicit role of government outlined above, government regulations impinge heavily on most of these economies, through setting state orders for key crops; contracting production and pricing arrangements for farmers with the state (notably in Turkmenistan and Uzbekistan); placing price controls on some products and services; controlling the sale and purchase of housing and industrial land; licensing and placing other requirements on the establishment of businesses and foreign investment; regulating wages and recruitment practices; putting restrictions on access to foreign exchange; requiring foreign trade registration with the commodities exchange; and imposing surrender requirements on export earnings.

Fiscal Adjustment Policies

Strategies to Reduce Fiscal Imbalances

Following independence, the Central Asian states experienced the loss of grants and other revenue from Russia. This development, in conjunction with the sharp output declines at the outset of transition, quickly triggered unsustainable fiscal deficits.[4] The need for fiscal adjustment to complement monetary stabilization became particularly apparent when the Central Asian states introduced their national currencies after the collapse of the ruble zone in 1993. Subsequent efforts to reduce fiscal deficits and contain inflationary pressures followed a bumpy road. Fiscal adjustment was, in most instances, repeatedly undermined by deteriorating revenue performance associated with the transition. The decline in revenue (ranging from 7 percentage points of GDP in Kazakhstan to 30 percentage points of GDP in Turkmenistan during 1992–95) reflected, for the most part, falling output, poor performance of state enterprises, and difficulties in adjusting tax policies and administration to the needs of a growing private sector. While strenuous efforts were made to suppress

---

[2]These credits, which mainly finance grain producers, are mostly interest-free and often not fully repaid by the recipients.

[3]As of 1999, the budget nominally includes external debt service obligations on government-guaranteed loans, which are serviced by the various state funds.

[4]The exception was Turkmenistan, which was initially shielded from much of the pain of adjustment by revenue from gas sales, before it lost access to European markets for gas exports as of 1993.

expenditure, attempts to protect certain spending categories and unforeseen events frequently resulted in a buildup of payments arrears. In periods of scarce budgetary funds, governments contributed to arrears by not paying for purchases of goods and services and writing off such nonpayments against tax arrears by the creditor entities (as happened on a large scale in Turkmenistan in 1997 and 1998). These actions postponed the problem and considerably weakened the transparency of government operations. The Central Asian states, therefore, experienced a start-stop fiscal adjustment—particularly at the outset of transition—with periods of progress interspersed with periods of reversal, and often marked by bank-financed clearances of accumulated payments arrears. The countries also could not adequately protect expenditure in social areas such as health and education, resulting in adverse consequences for human resource development.

Notwithstanding the uneven approaches adopted, most of the countries in the region have achieved underlying structural improvements in their fiscal accounts since independence. The two most successful cases of fiscal consolidation—Kazakhstan and the Kyrgyz Republic—have been aided by ongoing IMF- and World Bank-supported program requirements, which have included major structural reforms, notably in the fiscal area. Successful implementation of reform programs have, in turn, assisted these countries in obtaining foreign financing. Uzbekistan's experience was marked by swings in fiscal policy. Some initial progress was made in fiscal adjustment—again within a program context—before fiscal policy was eased considerably in 1996. The budget deficit was contained at about 2 percent of GDP during 1997–98, although this was primarily achieved by shifting the burden of directed low-interest credits back to commercial banks. The task of fiscal adjustment in Tajikistan was complicated by civil strife and natural disasters, although an ongoing IMF-supported arrangement has started to yield results in 1997 and 1998. In Turkmenistan, the urgency for fiscal adjustment was masked, until recently, by the very narrow coverage of the general government budget, which was balanced during 1996–97. In 1998, however, the fiscal situation deteriorated following the discontinuation of gas exports in the preceding year and the granting of large budgetary wage increases. The country has also tended to resist official involvement of multilateral agencies in program design, instead opting for its own approach to stabilization and structural reform.

Table 4.1 summarizes the fiscal cash deficits in the general government sectors of the Central Asian states and the financing of these deficits from foreign and domestic banking sources. Although the data suffer from weaknesses and may not be strictly comparable across countries, it appears that all countries in the region (with the exception of Uzbekistan in 1996 and Turkmenistan in 1998) were successful in reducing reliance on domestic bank financing of their fiscal deficits during 1996–98. Notwithstanding some common trends, the fiscal adjustment experiences of the individual countries in question varied considerably.

Kazakhstan's fiscal adjustment effort began in earnest in 1995, underpinned by a number of structural reforms, including the introduction of a modern tax code. The budget deficit—which had peaked at 7½ percent of GDP in the preceding year because of poor revenue performance and a mismanaged initiative to clear interenterprise arrears—was reduced to 3 percent of GDP. The deficit increased again in 1996, partly due to the adverse revenue impact of reforms in external trade taxation. In 1997 the deficit reached almost 7 percent of GDP, partly the result of a public investment program developed with international assistance, but it also reflected the clearance of pension arrears and reductions in other expenditure arrears. Important structural reforms in taxation and the social safety net were introduced during the year, including the adoption of legislation on a new pension scheme (see Section VIII). A Eurobond issue helped contain domestic bank financing of the budget. The deficit continued to be high in 1998, partly because of the costs of the pension reform that took effect on January 1, 1998. The credibility of Kazakhstan's reform program allowed it to obtain foreign credits from 1995 through 1998. This became more difficult in the wake of the financial crisis in Russia in 1998, after which a planned Eurobond issue was postponed.

The fiscal stabilization experience of the Kyrgyz Republic bore a number of similarities to that of Kazakhstan. The initial push to reduce the fiscal deficit began after the introduction of the national currency in May 1993. With revenue falling relative to GDP, fiscal restraint in the 1994 budget owed much to expenditure compression, including the elimination of a bread subsidy and other subsidies, but also to a buildup of payments arrears exceeding 4 percent of GDP. While the fiscal deficit, on a cash basis, declined from 14 percent of GDP in 1993 to 12 percent in 1994, there was a sharp reversal in 1995, largely because of a considerable weakening in revenue performance. A sizable reduction in the cash deficit was targeted for 1996, with revenue collections expected to benefit from the adoption of a new tax code and expenditure to be contained by means of scaling back health and education outlays, a tightening in the eligibility for social transfers, and suspension of a scheduled wage increase. Once again, a disappointing revenue performance upset budgetary strategy and the deficit reached 10 percent of GDP. The fiscal situation improved only marginally

Table 4.1. Fiscal Indicators
(In percent of GDP)

	1993	1994	1995	1996	1997	1998 Prov.
General Government Revenue[1]						
Kazakhstan[2]	21	18	17	13	13	14
Kyrgyz Republic	25	21	17	16	16	18
Tajikistan[3]	...	...	15	12	14	12
Turkmenistan	23	10	12	17	25	20
Uzbekistan	36	29	35	34	31	32
General Government Expenditure						
Kazakhstan[3]	25	26	20	18	20	22
Kyrgyz Republic	39	32	33	25	25	27
Tajikistan	...	...	26	18	17	16
Turkmenistan	23	11	14	17	25	23
Uzbekistan	46	35	39	41	33	34
General Government Balance (– deficit)[4]						
Kazakhstan[3]	–4	–8	–3	–5	–7	–8
Kyrgyz Republic[5]	–14	–12	–17	–10	–9	–9
Tajikistan	–25	–11	–11	–6	–3	–4
Turkmenistan	0	–1	–2	0	0	–3
Uzbekistan	–10	–6	–4	–7	–2	–2
Of which						
Foreign Financing (net)						
Kazakhstan	0	2	2	3	3	3
Kyrgyz Republic[5]	13	10	9	7	8	9
Tajikistan	...	...	0	3	2	3
Turkmenistan	0	0	0	0	–1	0
Uzbekistan	...	0	2	0	0	0
Domestic Bank Financing						
Kazakhstan	1	3	1	0	1	1
Kyrgyz Republic	2	2	8	3	1	1
Tajikistan	25	10	11	3	2	1
Turkmenistan	0	1	2	0	1	3
Uzbekistan	...	5	2	7	1	0

Sources: National authorities; and IMF staff estimates.

[1]Including grants.

[2]State budget; excludes privatization receipts.

[3]State budget only.

[4]Government expenditure minus revenue. The difference between the fiscal balance and the financing identified in this table is covered by privatization receipts (Kazakhstan) and nonbank financing.

[5]The Kyrgyz Republic budget expenditures and deficits shown here include the externally financed Public Investment Program, which amounted to 4 percent of GDP in 1994 and 1995, 3 percent of GDP in 1996 and 1997, and 5 percent of GDP in 1998.

during 1997–98, as expenditure was boosted by foreign-financed investment projects. Like Kazakhstan, the credibility of its reform program allowed the Kyrgyz Republic to borrow abroad,[5] which helped to limit domestic bank financing of the budget. Excluding foreign-financed investment projects, the primary budget recorded a deficit of less than 2 percent of GDP in 1998, down from over 13 percent of GDP in 1995, reflecting a sharp, across-the-board reduction in expenditures.

Fiscal adjustment in Uzbekistan was also uneven, notwithstanding a relatively strong revenue performance, attributable mainly to a smaller output decline. The less precarious revenue situation reflected less strict budget constraints imposed on the still predominantly state-owned enterprises, as well as lack of reform in other areas (i.e., the maintenance of restrictions on cash withdrawals from

---

[5]In the case of the Kyrgyz Republic, borrowing abroad was from official bilateral and multilateral sources on concessional terms.

banks). The general government recorded a deficit of 10 percent of GDP in 1993 due to very sharp expenditure growth, while revenue performance remained strong. Within the framework of an adjustment program supported by the IMF, the deficit was reduced to about 4 percent of GDP by 1995, largely through expenditure compression. Progress was set back in 1996 (with the deficit rebounding to 7 percent of GDP) in the wake of policy reversals and large net lending from the budget as part of an operation to clear payments arrears. The adoption of a number of new tax measures and maintenance of relatively tight expenditure controls through sequestration and sizable cuts in net lending—as subsidized lending was moved back to commercial banks—held the cash deficit to about 2 percent of GDP in 1997 and 1998. In the absence of foreign financing over the past three years, the budget deficit has been financed mainly through domestic bank credit and the purchase of treasury bills by state-owned enterprises.

Although Turkmenistan's fiscal reform effort since independence has been limited (for example, its tax structure has not changed substantially from that of the original Soviet system), it has seemingly avoided fiscal deficits. Interpretation of the fiscal position, which was nearly balanced during 1993–97, is complicated by the partial coverage of the general government budget and the existence of sizable quasi-fiscal deficits financed through public financial institutions by means of government-mandated directed credits. Less than 50 percent of current public sector transactions seem to pass through the formal budget. As most extrabudgetary spending is financed by external borrowing, the actual public sector deficit (which would include the quasi-fiscal operations of nonfinancial public enterprises) is, in all probability, considerably larger than what is captured in the official budget or reflected in domestic credit data.[6] With the suspension of gas sales to traditional markets in 1997 (resumed in early 1999), large consecutive wage increases granted to budgetary organizations, and heavy public spending on construction, the budget deficit deteriorated in 1998 to about 3 percent of GDP, intensifying the pressure on banking system resources. The authorities increasingly recognize the need to develop a coherent plan of action—encompassing all aspects of tax and expenditure policy, as well as institutional capacity building in the area of financial and tax administration—to deal with the deteriorating fiscal situation. The government is also now attempting to monitor a broader public sector (as opposed to the narrow bud-

get) by nominally including the state funds, some price subsidies, and foreign debt repayments on budget, although these operations do not go through the treasury accounts.

Tajikistan's fiscal adjustment effort showed variations over the period reviewed, as in the other four states of the region. In the earlier years, fiscal policy was characterized by weak tax administration and poor expenditure controls. Notwithstanding a decline in revenue arising from policy changes, which reduced revenue from the key agricultural subsectors (including cotton), the fiscal deficit was sharply reduced in 1996. This was attributable to a massive contraction in the expenditure to GDP ratio, attributable partly to the replacement of the generalized bread subsidy with targeted assistance. As in the other Central Asian states, curtailment of spending brought with it a sharp rise in payment arrears. The problems were compounded by the absence of a centralized treasury capable of documenting and controlling commitments. The post-conflict program initiated in 1997 with IMF support, and followed by an Enhanced Structural Adjustment Facility in 1998, was marked by strong fiscal adjustment, reflecting both revenue measures and improved tax compliance, which enabled progress in eliminating payments arrears. The strengthening of revenue has become more essential, given the need for government expenditure to grow, as a share of GDP, to support improvements in the provision of basic services, rebuild damaged infrastructure, and enhance the social safety net.

The Arrears Problem

All of the Central Asian states experienced significant tax arrears during the transition period and, partly linked to this, incurred large government payments arrears. Government payments arrears became a natural offset to tax arrears. Although these developments mostly mirrored weak state enterprise profitability, there was also a lack of financial discipline among enterprise managers and a failure by the government, as the sole shareholder, to impose hard budget constraints on enterprises. The elimination of tax arrears required enterprise managers to play a more active role in ensuring timely payments, and tax administrations to employ firmer approaches in identifying and collecting overdue taxes. Resolution of the expenditure arrears problem called for the preparation of more realistic initial budget estimates. Beyond this, however, the development of treasury operations, capable of monitoring cash payments against commitments and taking quick action to prevent new arrears from arising, was a crucial element in addressing the problem. Finally, it was essential for governments and central banks to refrain from fi-

---

[6]For example, for the first time, the 1999 budget shows the costs (estimated at about 2 percent of GDP) associated with the free provision of gas, electricity, and water to domestic users.

nancially bailing out enterprises persistently in arrears, as such action perpetuated the problem by creating expectations of future bailouts.

The most concerted attempt to reduce expenditure arrears in the region, occurred in Kazakhstan where the central government repaid almost its entire stock of wage and utility arrears at the end of 1996. Arrears at the local government level, together with pension and other payments arrears, however, would have reached about 5 percent of GDP by end-1997 in the absence of measures to clear them. As noted earlier, the authorities repaid pension arrears corresponding to about 2 percent of GDP, in preparation for the introduction of a pension reform, and reduced other expenditure arrears by about 1 percent of GDP during 1997. The authorities intended to clear the remaining arrears during the subsequent two years, but only a limited further reduction could be achieved in 1998 due to the tight fiscal situation. The Kyrgyz Republic also employed an active approach to eliminate arrears, aided by the creation of a strong central treasury and substantive improvements in tax administration. Nevertheless, weaknesses in expenditure management resurfaced during 1998, especially after the onset of the crisis in Russia. Tajikistan, Turkmenistan, and Uzbekistan continue to have substantial tax and expenditure arrears. Turkmenistan has an operational treasury, although the data processing systems in place do not provide timely information on commitments, making it difficult for the authorities to measure and to phase out payments arrears. Treasuries are only now being created in Uzbekistan and Tajikistan, which will help build a capacity to monitor payments arrears. Tajikistan has already made considerable progress by clearing budgetary wage and pension arrears by end-1998. In all five countries, addressing the government expenditure arrears problem will require progress in reducing tax arrears, as these two categories largely serve to offset one another.

Areas for Further Improvement

Fiscal adjustment measures implemented thus far in the Central Asian states constitute the initial steps of a reform agenda that still has a considerable way to go toward completion. With regard to revenue, policies will need to be directed toward broadening the tax base, unifying tax rates, and reducing tax exemptions. Key products, such as oil and gas, will need to be subjected to the full tax regime, while mechanisms are put in place to ensure that the rent associated with exploitation of natural resources is adequately taxed (principally through royalties). The tax status of small businesses and individuals will need to be reconsidered, so that reasonable contributions are obtained, while prohibitive and discouraging marginal tax rates are avoided. Such rates not only encourage a shift of activities to the informal economy, but also reduce the supply of labor and capital of those whose activity is taxed. A revenue mix that imposes unduly high social service and payroll taxes on enterprises (thus discouraging employment), while allowing individuals relatively small contributions, will need to be avoided. Tax administration is underdeveloped in most Central Asian states, and there is a need to strengthen procedures to assess, collect, and record tax payments. More effective enforcement methods, plus internal control and accountability systems, are also needed.

With regard to expenditure, it will be important to more clearly delineate the respective roles of the public and private sectors in the Central Asian states, including defining the role of enterprises that remain under state control. There is a need to adjust the expenditure mix, with some reduction in the still excessive spending on subsidies, and greater attention paid to spending on health and education. At the same time, spending needs to be made more cost effective through improved design. For example, in the areas of health and education, inefficiencies stemming from overstaffing and excess physical capacity have to be addressed. Also, social safety nets would benefit from closer targeting to vulnerable groups. To implement these reforms, the institutional capacity of the ministries of finance need to be strengthened. While creation of treasuries capable of strong sequestration controls have proved useful in the initial phase of transition, these steps should be bolstered by better identification of essential spending programs and measures to enhance cost effectiveness.

Bibliography

Chand, Sheetal K., and Henri R. Lorie, 1992, "Fiscal Policy," in *Fiscal Policies in Economies in Transition*, ed. by Vito Tanzi (Washington: International Monetary Fund).

Cheasty, Adrienne, and Jeffrey M. Davis, 1996, "Fiscal Transition in Countries of the Former Soviet Union: An Interim Assessment," IMF Working Paper 96/61 (Washington: International Monetary Fund).

Ebrill, Liam, and Oleh Havrylyshyn, 1999, *Tax Reform in the Baltics, Russia, and Other Countries of the Former Soviet Union*, IMF Occasional Paper No. 182 (Washington: International Monetary Fund).

Hemming, Richard, Adrienne Cheasty, and Ashok K. Lahiri, 1995, "The Revenue Decline," in *Policy Experiences and Issues in the Baltics, Russia, and Other Countries of the Former Soviet Union*, ed. by Daniel A. Citrin and Ashok K. Lahiri, IMF Occasional Paper No. 133 (Washington: International Monetary Fund).

International Monetary Fund, 1996, "Fiscal Challenges of Transition: Progress Made and Problems Remaining," in *World Economic Outlook, May 1996*, World Economic and Financial Surveys (Washington).

———, World Bank, Organization for Economic Cooperation and Development, European Bank for Reconstruction and Development, 1991, *A Study of the Soviet Economy*, Vol. 1 (Washington: International Monetary Fund).

Tanzi, Vito, 1993, "Fiscal Policy and the Economic Restructuring of Economies in Transition," IMF Working Paper 93/22 (Washington: International Monetary Fund).

V   Monetary Policy and Progress with Stabilization

Harry Snoek and Ron van Rooden

Following independence in 1991, the states of the former Soviet Union continued to operate essentially within the framework of the monetary and financial system inherited from the Soviet era.[1] The Central Bank of Russia took over the role of the now defunct Gosbank as the bank of emission, and the newly independent states continued to use the ruble as their currency. To many of the countries, the main attraction of being a part of the ruble area was the possibility of continued access to Central Bank of Russia credit to finance trade deficits with Russia. In January 1992, the Central Bank of Russia established correspondent accounts with the central banks of the individual states through which it provided credit, thus supplying rubles to settle interstate payments. The individual central banks also established correspondent accounts bilaterally.

Introduction of National Currencies

The loss of access to rubles in July 1993 confronted the Central Asian states with a choice between subordinating monetary policy to Russia under a new ruble area controlled by the Central Bank of Russia or gaining full autonomy in the pursuit of their own stabilization policies. The Central Asian states opted to pursue their own policies, albeit with differing degrees of enthusiasm and urgency.

The Kyrgyz Republic took the lead in using a new domestic currency by introducing the som in May 1993 and adopting a floating exchange rate (Table 5.1). Kazakhstan and Uzbekistan, instead, signed an agreement with Russia in August 1993, establishing a new ruble area under Central Bank of Russia control, which later included Tajikistan, Armenia, and Belarus. Uncertainties about the workings of the new system triggered large disturbances in domestic financial markets. In November 1993, Kazakhstan and Uzbekistan reneged on the new ruble area. On November 15, Kazakhstan introduced the tenge

under a floating exchange rate regime, and Uzbekistan introduced the sum-coupon,[2] initially pegging it to the ruble at par. Turkmenistan, which did not rely on Central Bank of Russia credits, given its large trade surplus (mostly gas related), also introduced its own currency, the manat, in November 1993. Tajikistan opted for a dual arrangement, continuing to use the cash ruble—which was provided by Russia on strict commercial terms—while at the same time creating noncash (deposit) rubles through the National Bank of Tajikistan. As the supply of noncash rubles increased much faster than cash rubles, the values of cash versus deposit rubles deviated and cash shortages emerged. Finally, under a broad currency reform, Tajikistan introduced the Tajik ruble in May 1995.

Conduct of Monetary Policy

Macroeconomic Situations Prior to Reforms

The transition period witnessed sharp deteriorations in the macroeconomic situations of the Central Asian states. Disruptions in trade patterns and increases in trade prices triggered large external current account deficits (except in Turkmenistan, which benefited from sharp price increases for natural gas exports), ranging in 1993 from under 10 percent of GDP in Kazakhstan and Uzbekistan to 16 percent of GDP in the Kyrgyz Republic, and to 31 percent of GDP in Tajikistan (Table 5.2). In the Kyrgyz Republic and Tajikistan, growing external deficits partly mirrored large fiscal deficits that were mainly associated with the withdrawal of transfers from the Soviet Union. While Turkmenistan and Uzbekistan had adequate international reserves, reflecting their strong external positions, reserves were low in Kazakhstan and the Kyrgyz Republic, and virtually nonexistent in Tajikistan.

The most striking indicators of worsening macroeconomic situations, however, were the very high

---

[1]For a detailed discussion of this system, see International Monetary Fund and others (1991), Vol. 2, pp. 107–35.

[2]The sum-coupon was replaced by the sum in July 1994.

Table 5.1. Introduction of National Currencies

	Date	Name	Currency reform / confiscation	Conversion rate	Exchange system at time of introduction of own currency	Remarks
Kazakhstan	November 15, 1993. Conversion period 6 days.	tenge	Individuals could convert cash up to Rub 100,000 (equal to the average monthly wage in October) and deposits existing before October 1 for the full amount; legal entities could convert cash up to 1.3 times the average balance held in July 1993. For both individuals and legal entities, amounts in excess of the limits had to be deposited and were released after proof of their legitimacy.	T 1 = Rub 500	Managed float through foreign exchange auctions.	The government imposed some administrative measures to prevent price increases because of conversion and to enforce acceptance. Also, restrictions on the use of cash were removed.
Kyrgyz Republic	May 10, 1993. Conversion period 5 days.	som	Savings deposits converted at som 1 = Rub 150 to compensate for inflation.	som 1 = Rub 200	Managed float through foreign exchange auctions.	
Tajikistan	May 10, 1995. No fixed conversion period; Russian rubles to continue to be used freely.	Tajik ruble	Cash and pre-1993 household deposits converted at TR 1=100 Rub; other deposits converted at TR 1=1,200 Rub but government and bank deposits converted at TR 1=1,000 Rub; bank credit converted at TR 1=1,000 Rub.	TR 1 = Rub 100	Managed float through foreign exchange auctions.	Remaining controlled prices liberalized or increased. Wage arrears converted into special blocked accounts, to be to be converted into privatization vouchers later. Most bank deposit and lending rates liberalized (except for priority sectors). Access to deposits liberalized for enterprises immediately and for households in July. Limits on holding of cash removed.
Turkmenistan	November 1, 1993.	manat	Banknotes in denominations of 5,000 and 10,000 rubles were withdrawn from circulation. Conversion of household deposits at manat 1 = Rub 500, but limited to September 1 balance with Savings Bank plus wage payments thereafter. Cash limited to Rub 30,000 per adult. Savings deposits with Savings Bank increased eightfold, but withdrawal only possible after January 1, 1994. Enterprise deposits converted at Rub 500 for a total amount of Rub 50 billion; 75% of remainder converted into bonds and 25% at manat 1 = Rub 500.	manat 1 = Rub 500	Managed float through foreign exchange auctions.	Additional reserve requirement of 20%.
Uzbekistan	November 15, 1993.	sum-coupon	Pre-1993 banknotes in denominations of 5,000 and 10,000 rubles no longer legal tender; banknotes of smaller denominations subsequently withdrawn. Households allowed to deposit Rub 200,000 in bank deposits, from which payments could be made. Deposits of over Rub 200,000 required to be placed in restricted noninterest bearing accounts.	SC 1 = Rub 1	Initially fixed at par with ruble, then managed float through foreign exchange auctions as of April 1994.	
	July 1, 1994.	sum	Restrictions on withdrawal of deposits continued.	sum 1 = SC 1,000	Managed float through foreign exchange auctions.	Preceded by restrictive monetary policy.

Source: International Monetary Fund.

rates of inflation in the Central Asian states. Confronted with enormous structural changes in their economies following the collapse of the Soviet Union, the overriding policy concern in the Central Asian states was to contain the impact of the adjustment on incomes. The newly established central banks heavily financed state enterprise losses and emerging government deficits. As a result, broad money grew dramatically in all cases—as much as fourfold in Uzbekistan and eightfold in Turkmenistan in 1992—and in most of the states (with the exception of the Kyrgyz Republic) at similar or higher rates in 1993 (Figure 5.1 and Table 5.3). Strong monetary growth, combined with price liberalization and moves toward world prices in interstate trade, led to a rapid acceleration in inflation. In 1992, inflation ranged from about 650 percent in Turkmenistan to almost 3,000 percent in Kazakhstan. In 1993, inflation remained at over 2,000 percent in Kazakhstan, accelerated to 1,400 percent in Turkmenistan and to 7,000 percent in Tajikistan, while declining to around 700 and 800 percent in the Kyrgyz Republic and Uzbekistan.

Implementation of Stabilization Policies and Initial Results

In all five Central Asian states, the ultimate objective of governments was to restore growth and to raise the living standards of the population. There were, however, differing degrees of recognition of the need for stabilization as a precondition for sustained growth. As of 1993, Kazakhstan and the Kyrgyz Republic maintained stabilization as an overriding policy objective, while Turkmenistan and Uzbekistan generally strove to spur employment and output growth by supporting state enterprises in ways that were inflationary and impeded growth. Tajikistan's situation was complicated by political difficulties and the military conflict, so that policy priorities were less clear in the initial period of transition.

The stabilization efforts of the five Central Asian states are detailed in Box 5.1. Kazakhstan and the Kyrgyz Republic stand out as the pioneers of economic reform in this group, and have progressed the most in achieving stabilization and growth. In the Kyrgyz Republic, inflation declined sharply to under 100 percent in 1994, the first year of the stabilization program. In Kazakhstan, there was a setback in early 1994 due to the monetization of interenterprise arrears, but a renewed emphasis on stabilization reduced inflation sharply to 60 percent by end-1995. Uzbekistan delayed implementing a stabilization program until after replacing the sum-coupon with the sum in mid-1994, but succeeded in bringing inflation under control by mid-1995. In Turkmenistan,

as of 1996, monetary policy was directed at reducing inflation, mainly by offsetting the expansionary impact of directed credits with stepped-up foreign exchange sales, and inflation declined rapidly thereafter to about 20 percent by end-1998. Tajikistan's experience was more turbulent. A monetary-based stabilization effort following the introduction of the Tajik ruble in mid-1995 was aborted by excessive bank credit to the government and state enterprises. A subsequent, more comprehensive stabilization program sharply lowered inflation in 1996 to about 40 percent, although there was a reversal in 1997 as policies lapsed during intensified civil conflict. Inflation was reduced sharply to 3 percent in 1998 as financial policies were once again tightened.

There were essentially two basic phases to reform. Notwithstanding unstable monetary relationships, the first phase relied primarily on monetary targeting, supported by strengthened fiscal discipline (mainly through expenditure restraint) and flexible exchange rate arrangements. In this phase, interest rates also moved toward positive real levels and directed (preferential) credits were discontinued. In the subsequent phase of stabilization, the exchange rate played an important role in sustaining the gains achieved and served as an indicator for the appropriateness of macroeconomic policies. Although floating exchange rate regimes were outwardly sustained in most cases, the exchange rates under these systems were effectively stabilized under a managed float by the central banks of the states. In addition, there was greater emphasis on speeding progress with structural reforms—notably public enterprise restructuring and privatization, tax reform, and financial sector reform—as an essential input into firming stabilization gains and setting the conditions for sustained growth. Among the faster reformers, Kazakhstan maintained a pragmatic approach to using monetary and exchange rate anchors for stabilization, while it further reduced fiscal and external imbalances and directed efforts at pushing forward with structural reforms. As a result, since 1996 it has had the lowest inflation rate of the five Central Asian states (less than 2 percent in 1998). Although the Kyrgyz Republic essentially continued to pursue money-based stabilization, exchange rate and external competitiveness considerations played an increasing role in policy formulation, while emphasis continued to be placed on structural reforms. Among the slower reformers, Turkmenistan and Uzbekistan, the exchange rate became an increasingly important indicator for stabilization. Both countries resorted to nonmarket-related measures, however, to maintain their official exchange rates, at the expense of sustaining sizable and recently widening gaps with parallel market rates.

Following the financial crisis in Russia in August 1998, however, exchange rates came under

Table 5.2. Selected Macroeconomic Indicators

	1992	1993	1994	1995	1996	1997	1998 Prov.
Kazakhstan							
Inflation (end-period; 12-month percentage change)	2,962.8	2,169.1	1,160.3	60.4	28.6	11.3	1.9
Real growth (percentage change)	−5.3	−9.2	−12.6	−8.2	0.5	1.7	−2.5
Exchange rate (end-of-period; domestic currency / US dollar)	...	6.3	54.3	64.0	73.9	75.9	84.9
Fiscal deficit (in percent of GDP)	−7.3	−4.1	−7.7	−3.2	−5.3	−7.0	−7.7
Current account balance (in percent of GDP)	−51.4	−9.4	−8.6	−3.1	−3.6	−4.1	−5.6
Gross official reserves (in months of imports)	0.2	1.3	2.6	2.7	3.1	3.2	3.0
Kyrgyz Republic							
Inflation (end-period; 12-month percentage change)	1,257.0	766.9	95.7	32.3	34.9	14.7	18.4
Real growth (percentage change)	−13.9	−15.5	−20.1	−5.4	7.1	9.9	2.0
Exchange rate (end-of-period; domestic currency / US dollar)	...	8.0	10.6	11.2	16.7	17.4	29.4
Fiscal deficit (in percent of GDP)	−17.0	−14.4	−11.6	−17.3	−9.5	−9.0	−8.8
Current account balance (in percent of GDP)	−10.6	−16.4	−11.2	−16.3	−23.5	−7.9	−16.7
Gross official reserves (in months of imports)	0.8	1.5	2.6	2.5	1.6	3.0	2.6
Tajikistan							
Inflation (end-period; 12-month percentage change)	...	7,343.7	1.1	2,135.2	40.5	163.6	2.7
Real growth (percentage change)	−29.0	−11.0	−21.5	−12.5	−4.4	1.7	5.3
Exchange rate (end-of-period; domestic currency / US dollar)[1]	415.0	1,247.0	3,550.0	293.5	328.0	748.0	977.0
Fiscal deficit (in percent of GDP)	−30.5	−25.0	−10.5	−11.2	−5.8	−3.3	−3.8
Current account balance (in percent of GDP)	−18.0	−30.7	−20.5	−14.6	−7.4	−5.5	−10.3
Gross official reserves (in months of imports)	0.0	0.0	0.0	0.1	0.2	0.6	1.3
Turkmenistan							
Inflation (end-period; 12-month percentage change)	644.0	1,400.0	1,328.5	1,261.5	445.9	21.4	19.8
Real growth (percentage change)	−5.3	−10.2	−19.0	−8.2	−7.7	−25.9	4.8
Exchange rate (end-of-period; domestic currency / US dollar)[2]	...	2.0	75.0	200.0	4,070.0	4,165.0	5,200.0
Fiscal deficit (in percent of GDP)	13.0	0.0	−1.0	−2.0	0.0	0.0	−3.0
Current account balance (in percent of GDP)	54.7	20.1	1.8	1.3	2.1	−27.3	−36.2
Gross official reserves (in months of imports)	0.0	6.2	6.6	8.5	9.2	15.3	14.6
Uzbekistan							
Inflation (end-period; 12-month percentage change)	910.0	884.8	1,281.4	116.9	64.4	50.2	26.1
Real growth (percentage change)	−11.0	−2.3	−4.2	−0.9	1.6	2.4	2.8
Exchange rate (end-of-period; domestic currency / US dollar)[2]	...	1.3	25.0	35.5	55.0	80.2	110.0
Fiscal deficit (in percent of GDP)	−18.0	−10.0	−6.1	−4.1	−7.3	−2.4	−2.3
Current account balance (in percent of GDP)	−11.7	−7.8	2.1	−0.2	−7.2	−4.0	−1.8
Gross official reserves (in months of imports)	0.6	3.8	5.9	6.9	5.4	3.7	5.0

Source: National authorities.
[1]Until 1994, Russian rubles; as of 1995, Tajik rubles.
[2]Official rate.

pressure and foreign investors reevaluated the risks of financing countries in the region. Indeed, risk premiums on interest rates increased and access to both domestic and foreign financing fell sharply; demand for Kazakh and Kyrgyz domestic-currency-denominated assets plummeted. Policy re-sponses differed among the Central Asian countries. At first, Kazakhstan, the Kyrgyz Republic, and Tajikistan allowed some depreciation of their currencies, combined with heavy intervention. In each case, intervention was supported by a tightening of fiscal and monetary policies, including

Figure 5.1. Monetary Growth and Inflation
(In percent)

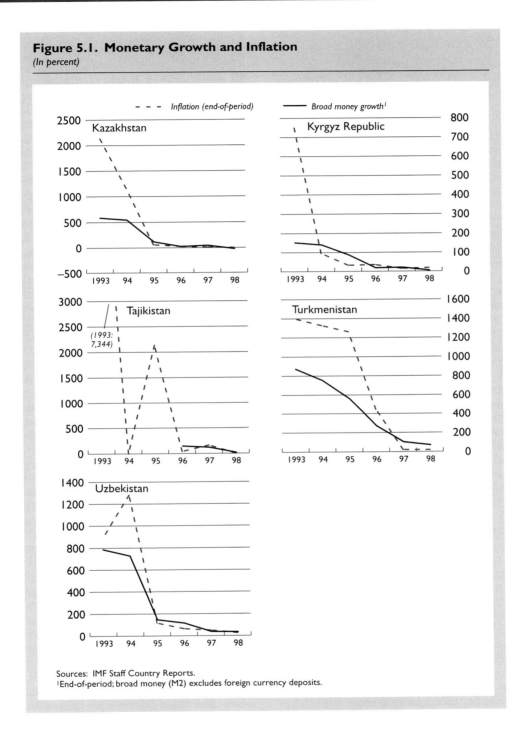

Sources: IMF Staff Country Reports.
[1] End-of-period; broad money (M2) excludes foreign currency deposits.

higher interest rates. In Kazakhstan the authorities were able to prevent a significant depreciation in the remainder of 1998, albeit at the cost of sizable intervention, but the Kyrgyz Republic and Tajikistan switched to a policy of minimal intervention, permitting their currencies to depreciate at a faster pace in order to allow exchange rates to find their own new levels. Uzbekistan and Turkmenistan, on the other hand, responded mainly by intensifying exchange restrictions, rather than tightening monetary and fiscal policies. As a result, while official exchange rates remained more or less stable, exchange rates in parallel markets depreciated sharply.

Table 5.3. Selected Monetary Indicators
(End-of-year percentage changes unless otherwise indicated)

	1993	1994	1995	1996	1997	1998 Prov.
Kazakhstan						
Reserve money	1,432.8	634.6	91.8	26.5	32.2	−23.8
Broad money (M2)[1]	581.0	540.2	113.7	20.9	41.9	−25.0
Currency in circulation	...	792.5	136.9	30.9	47.7	−25.9
Currency to deposit ratio[2]	0.5	0.9	1.2	1.5	1.4	1.4
Velocity[3]	2.0	7.2	8.3	10.1	10.6	12.2
Inflation	2,169.1	1,160.3	60.4	28.6	11.3	1.9
Kyrgyz Republic						
Reserve money	...	104.7	91.4	23.9	21.1	6.8
Broad money (M2)[1]	151.3	139.6	86.9	17.9	20.4	4.9
Currency in circulation	264.5	207.2	93.4	23.8	11.7	6.9
Currency to deposit ratio[2]	0.2	0.2	0.3	4.4	3.1	3.2
Velocity[3]	8.5	8.4	6.0	7.3	7.0	7.2
Inflation	766.9	95.7	32.3	34.9	14.7	18.4
Tajikistan[4]						
Reserve money	1,600.3	115.9	...	139.5	193.5	4.9
Broad money (M2)[1]	...	...	...	142.6	117.2	14.8
Currency in circulation	...	...	...	184.7	137.5	24.8
Currency to deposit ratio[2]	...	...	1.6	2.7	3.9	6.9
Velocity[3]	...	...	7.3	14.3	13.4	19.1
Inflation	7,343.7	1.1	2,135.2	40.5	163.6	2.7
Turkmenistan						
Reserve money	...	919.0	517.2	348.3	49.9	112.2
Broad money (M2)[1]	871.7	753.1	560.5	269.8	101.8	70.0
Currency in circulation	3,457.7	827.6	560.0	377.2	50.9	155.1
Currency to deposit ratio[2]	0.8	1.0	1.0	1.7	0.9	2.4
Velocity[3]	8.1	10.3	10.8	21.5	14.0	9.8
Inflation	1,400.0	1,328.5	1,261.5	445.9	21.4	19.8
Uzbekistan						
Reserve money	...	476.2	194.3	112.1	18.4	39.9
Broad money (M2)[1]	784.0	726.2	144.3	113.3	36.0	33.0
Currency in circulation	505.2	480.0	183.8	152.5	38.6	43.3
Currency to deposit ratio[2]	0.3	0.5	0.6	0.8	0.8	0.9
Velocity[3]	4.2	6.8	8.5	7.1	8.0	8.3
Inflation	884.8	1,281.4	116.9	64.4	50.2	26.1

Sources: National authorities; and IMF staff estimates.

[1]Excluding foreign currency deposits.

[2]Ratio of currency to deposits denominated in domestic currency.

[3]Ratio of GDP to end-period broad money (excluding foreign currency deposits).

[4]The introduction of the Tajik ruble in 1995, with different conversion rates for different types of deposit, precludes comparison of 1995 data with the previous year.

Factors Affecting Money Demand

The demand for money in the Central Asian states has generally remained low, notwithstanding recent stabilization gains, reflecting continued lack of confidence in the currencies. Monetary policy in these countries targeted monetary aggregates. Slower growth in these aggregates was expected to lower inflation, restore confidence, and affect real sector variables in the desired direction. In all five Central Asian states, money demand declined rapidly in the first year after the introduction of the new currencies. This was reflected in a sharp increase in velocity as the public increasingly shifted into goods and foreign exchange. The demand for money recovered only very gradually following macroeconomic improvements, hampered in some cases by intensifying problems in banking systems.

Lack of confidence in the currencies was also reflected in the growing share of foreign currency de-

Box 5.1. Stabilization Policies in the Central Asian States

Kazakhstan adopted a comprehensive stabilization and reform program following the introduction of the tenge in late 1993, with monetary targets serving as nominal anchors. Large credits were extended to clear interenterprise arrears, however, and little progress was made in reducing the fiscal and current account deficits. Monetary policy was subsequently tightened, assisted by measures to reduce the fiscal deficit. Following a surge in capital inflows in 1995, monetary targets again gained primacy. The National Bank of Kazakhstan engaged in sterilization operations, while some nominal appreciation of the exchange rate was allowed. Stabilization efforts were further challenged in 1996 when a banking crisis eroded confidence in the tenge. Central bank sales of foreign exchange absorbed excess liquidity and helped stabilize the exchange rate. Improvements in the fiscal and external positions during 1995–96 solidified the stabilization gains. By 1998, inflation was reduced to 2 percent.

The **Kyrgyz Republic** also adopted a money-based stabilization program in 1993, which was derailed when sizable credits were extended to finance the agricultural sector and public enterprises. Monetary policy was subsequently tightened and overall credit growth in the economy almost came to a standstill in 1994 as banks were instructed to stop lending to state enterprises in financial difficulties. By March 1995, monthly inflation declined to about 1 percent. This policy stance was broadly continued in the subsequent period, although periodic sharp increases in central bank credit to the government (reflecting expansionary fiscal policies in late 1995 and, again, in late 1996 in connection with elections) and depreciations of the exchange rate led to temporary surges in inflation. Since January 1998, the central bank has no longer been allowed to extend credit to the government. Monthly inflation increased in late 1998 following the financial crisis in Russia, which resulted in a sharp depreciation of the exchange rate.

In **Tajikistan**, inflation surged in 1993 as pre-1993 rubles, which continued to be legal tender, streamed in from neighboring countries. Inflation declined following a currency reform and the imposition of severe restrictions on cash withdrawals in 1994, but rebounded in early 1995 reflecting an easing in monetary policy. The stabilization program following the introduction of the Tajik ruble in May 1995 was money-based. However, excessive bank credit to the government and enterprises

led to hyperinflation in the second half of the year. A more comprehensive stabilization and reform program introduced in early 1996 initially succeeded in lowering inflation, but renewed political problems prevented a sustained implementation of the program and, once again, eroded the stabilization gains. Renewed efforts at stabilization resulted in a sharp lowering of inflation during 1998.

Turkmenistan failed to support the introduction of the manat with a comprehensive stabilization program. On the external side, a major policy objective was to increase international reserves, while monetary policy was geared to maintaining employment and incomes by providing preferential credits to enterprises. The first serious stabilization effort came in 1996, when a tighter monetary policy contributed to a slowdown in inflation. The lack of hard budget constraints on enterprises was, however, reflected in a large-scale resumption of directed credits in late 1996 and 1997. The central bank's efforts shifted to stabilizing the exchange rate by sharply increasing foreign exchange sales, financed partly by foreign borrowing. As a result, monthly inflation rates dropped below 3 percent as of February 1997. Monetary policy continues to be constrained by the absence of central bank control over international reserves (which remain under the president's control). In late 1998, monthly inflation increased to over 4 percent, following large directed credits and central bank financing of the budget.

Uzbekistan failed to adopt strong stabilization measures in conjunction with the introduction of the sum-coupon in late 1993. Large monetary expansion caused monthly inflation to remain at around 30–40 percent until mid-1994. A more comprehensive stabilization effort was made following the introduction of the sum. During the second half of 1994 and 1995, the authorities mainly targeted monetary aggregates. Inflation declined, although remaining higher than anticipated due to large unsterilized foreign exchange inflows. In the last quarter of 1996, sizable lending to the cotton sector was reflected in a rising bank-financed budget deficit, an acceleration in inflation, and a deterioration in the external current account. Foreign exchange restrictions were reimposed and dual exchange rates maintained, with a far more depreciated cash rate. Monetary policy was subsequently tightened, and monthly inflation declined to about 2 percent during 1998.

posits in broad money (M2, including foreign currency deposits), and the high ratio between currency in circulation and deposits denominated in domestic currency. The ratio of currency in circulation to M2 (excluding foreign currency deposits) is not only high in the Central Asian countries because of the underdeveloped payments systems, but has remained high also in those countries that have made

considerable progress in stabilization. In Kazakhstan, the Kyrgyz Republic, Turkmenistan, and Tajikistan, currency still accounted for 60–85 percent of M2 at end-1998. In Uzbekistan, currency in circulation accounted for about 50 percent of M2, but this can be attributed to restrictions on cash withdrawals. A tendency toward some strengthening in financial intermediation from late 1997 onward (notably in the Kyrgyz Republic) faced a setback in the aftermath of the crisis in Russia.

Impact of Capital Inflows

Similar to the experience of other transition economies, some of the Central Asian states witnessed sharp increases in capital inflows, which threatened their disinflation efforts.[3] This not only reflected the attraction of a more stable economic environment for foreign capital, but also some remonetization and reverse currency substitution by the population as confidence in the economies strengthened. The ensuing increase in domestic liquidity ran the risk of undermining the stabilization efforts under way, and delaying enterprise and bank restructuring by encouraging less prudent lending. The authorities were faced essentially with the choice of sterilizing the additional liquidity through sales of central bank or treasury bills (in excess of budgetary financing needs), further fiscal tightening, exchange rate appreciation, or a combination of these policies.

In Kazakhstan, strong capital inflows in the first half of 1995—associated with improved economic performance, but also with the granting of management contracts to foreign parties—threatened a rebound in inflation. The authorities' initial reaction was to offset the liquidity impact of the inflows by tightening monetary policy, including through sales of short-term central bank notes, while maintaining a stable exchange rate. When the inflows persisted, the focus of policies was shifted to attaining the monetary targets and allowing some appreciation of the exchange rate. In Uzbekistan, the central bank responded to a large increase in international reserves at end-1994 by tightening monetary policy, including through sales of central bank certificates of deposits and interventions in the interbank market. In both instances, policy choices were needed to weigh the potentially damaging effects of persistent exchange rate appreciation on export competitiveness against the desirability of allowing some exchange rate appreciation to help promote domestic price stability. Also, prolonged sterilization through sales of central bank notes carried quasi-fiscal costs and was likely to be constrained by the capacity of the local markets to absorb such sales. These issues are likely to be confronted by the other countries in the group as reforms progress. To the extent that a strengthening in the credibility of reform programs and sustained upturns in economic activity raise the real demand for money in these countries, increases in their money supplies associated with capital inflows could partly be accommodated without weakening

their disinflation efforts. Until that occurs, the fine tuning of policies in the face of capital inflows will be crucial to protecting stabilization gains.

Monetary Policy Reforms

The implementation of monetary policy in the Central Asian states was constrained by

- weak understanding of the role and the importance of an independent monetary policy, lack of experience by the newly formed central banks, and inadequacy of monetary policy instruments;
- a strong legacy from the Soviet period, when banks were merely administrators of money flows allocated under the plan, and hence an absence of adequate infrastructure and behavior patterns through which monetary signals could be transmitted;
- the ongoing restructuring of national banking systems and weaknesses in the legal and regulatory framework for banking activities; and
- low demand for money and widespread currency substitution, reflecting weak confidence in the newly introduced currencies fueled by instability in the years preceding their introduction, as well as a prevalent distrust of banks by the public, initially because of restrictions on deposit withdrawals and confiscatory elements in the currency reform measures, and later due to financial problems faced by banks.

Addressing these issues was important for the success of money-based stabilization policies.

Central Bank Independence and Monetary Policy Instruments

At the outset of transition, the Central Asian states mostly continued to give precedence to financing state enterprises and the government over attaining monetary targets. The countries in question inherited a two-tiered banking system from the Soviet Union, in which the central bank (under the 1990 Law of the State Bank of the U.S.S.R.) was responsible for maintaining stability of the currency.[4] The first stabilization efforts were derailed, however, mainly because of large central bank financing of enterprise losses and government deficits, as happened in the Kyrgyz Republic (1993), Kazakhstan (1994), and

---

[3]See Ize (1996).

[4]For a detailed analysis of central bank reform and monetary policy in transition economies, see Sundararajan, Petersen, and Sensenbrenner (1997), and de Melo and Denizer (1997).

Uzbekistan (end-1996). In subsequent, more successful stabilization programs, these slippages were addressed by reinforcing the autonomy of the central bank and making bolder moves to reduce the budget deficit and impose hard budget constraints on state enterprises. Hence, the Kyrgyz Republic gave wide-ranging autonomy to its central bank in implementing policies to reduce inflation and stabilize the exchange rate with the central bank law of 1992, while since 1998, direct National Bank of the Kyrgyz Republic financing of the budget is not allowed. Kazakhstan, in a new central bank law adopted in 1995 (Table 5.4), introduced the requirement that the need for central bank financing of the budget be specified in the budget document. As a result, central bank financing declined sharply in both countries. In the other three countries, however, government-mandated central bank credits to finance the budget, as well as priority sectors and enterprises, continued, undermining attainment of the monetary targets. A new central bank law adopted at the end of 1996 gave the National Bank of Tajikistan independence, but pressure on the bank for ad hoc financing continued, despite the issuance of a presidential decree in mid-1997 explicitly terminating such credits.

In order to improve the efficiency of credit allocation and move toward market-determined interest rates, starting in 1993, the Central Asian central banks gradually increased interest rates on their lending to market levels through credit auctions (except in Tajikistan, where this process began only in late 1997). In Kazakhstan and the Kyrgyz Republic, by mid-1994, virtually all central bank credit was channeled through auctions at market rates that were positive in real terms (Figure 5.2). In Uzbekistan, where interbank rather than central bank auctions were initiated, the central bank withdrew liquidity by buying credit in the auction in 1994–95, as large foreign exchange inflows increased liquidity in the banking system. As foreign capital inflows dried up in later years, banks became increasingly reliant on central bank financing, and interest rates again became essentially determined by the central bank. Turkmenistan's experience was less even. Credit auctions were suspended in early 1996 and the central bank continued to provide subsidized credit under government direction; an attempt to reinstate credit auctions in mid-1996 failed, as did a recent similar attempt. On balance, the credit auctions gave the central banks exposure to market-related instruments and encouraged commercial banks to develop alternative sources of financing. In Kazakhstan and the Kyrgyz Republic, the interbank credit market became, by 1995, a more important source of finance than the credit auctions. At the same time, the interbank market could be used for interventions in line with the monetary policy stance. As the credit auctions lost importance as sources of liquidity for banks, the central banks of Kazakhstan and the Kyrgyz Republic established separate Lombard and emergency facilities to provide short- or medium-term liquidity to banks.

A further step in increasing the mix of monetary policy instruments was the introduction of treasury bill auctions. Although such auctions were initiated in Kazakhstan and the Kyrgyz Republic during 1993–94, portfolios were initially too small to allow for open market operations. In order to increase the stock of tradable paper, the National Bank of Kazakhstan complemented treasury bills with its own short-term paper in June 1995. By mid-1996, it introduced repurchase and reverse repurchase transactions to regulate liquidity in the banking system. In the Kyrgyz Republic, central bank credit to the government was partially securitized by mid-1997, allowing the central bank to introduce repurchase and reverse repurchase operations in 1997; the credit auctions were officially stopped in January 1997. Treasury bill auctions in Uzbekistan did not start until 1996, although the Central Bank of Uzbekistan issued its own certificates of deposit in 1995. Turkmenistan started issuing treasury bills in July 1994, but the amounts issued by the ministry of economy and finance at fixed prices have remained relatively small, preventing their use for monetary policy purposes. There is no secondary market in treasury bills. Tajikistan has also made some progress in this area, with treasury bill auctions in limited amounts initiated in the latter part of 1998.

Interest Rate Policies

The Central Asian states (except Tajikistan) lifted interest rate controls on commercial banks during 1992–93. The central bank refinance rates in these countries, however, while more flexible than in the past, were often not adequately adjusted in line with inflation. Since central bank credit was a major source of finance for banks (on-lended at fixed spreads), interest rates remained negative in real terms. Also, in most countries, the ability of banks to accept deposits from individuals was limited (often to the bank's capital), so that the savings bank—whose rates were fixed by the authorities—had a virtual monopoly over deposits of individuals. Adjustments in deposit rates considerably lagged behind the rapid increase in inflation, resulting in increasing negative real rates.

In the years following the introduction of national currencies, however, interest rates became gradually more market determined in Kazakhstan, the Kyrgyz Republic, and initially in Uzbekistan (although this

Table 5.4. Central Bank Reform and Monetary Policy Instruments

	Central bank independence	Refinance rate	Credit to government	Credit to banks	Reserve requirement	Treasury bills	Other instruments
Kazakhstan	January 1993 constitution makes NBK independent, but under supervision of parliament. Under 1995 central bank law, NBK has considerable autonomy; extends credit to government only against treasury bills.	Set by NBK.	At treasury bill rate.	Credit auctions since January 1993, but replaced by open market type instruments in 1996. Interbank credit market started in April 1995.	Unified at 20 percent in November 1995, and reduced to 15 percent in July 1996, and to 10 percent in January 1998.	Treasury bill auctions started in December 1994.	Short-term NBK notes started in 1995; repurchase/ reverse repurchase orders in Treasury bills.
Kyrgyz Republic	1992 and 1998 laws give high degree of independence; no NBKR financing of budget effective January 1998.	Initially at credit auction rate; since 1994 at treasury bill rate, although discount rate set ad hoc by NBKR Board between August-November 1998.	At zero interest rate; no more credit to government effective January 1998.	Credit auctions started in February 1993; by 1994, all NBKR credit through market related instruments; interbank market more important role in bank financing in 1995; Lombard and last resort credit facility.	Requirement of 20 percent, reserves remunerated related first to auction rate then to treasury bill rate, since 1997 related to weighted average bank deposit rate. Sharply raised penalty rates for non-compliance in 1998.	Treasury bill auctions started in May 1993.	Repurchase/reverse repurchase orders started in 1997.
Tajikistan	1996 national bank law grants NBT independence and prohibits interference from government bodies.	Based on credit auction rate.	At zero interest rate.	Mainly through credit auctions.	Unified at 20 percent, no remuneration.	Started in July 1998.	None.
Turkmenistan	1993 national bank law grants little autonomy; quantity and cost of central bank credit decided by government. Automatic overdraft to government.	Set by CBT.	Interest-free overdraft; occasionally, long-term credit at rates established by the government (normally zero).	Mainly through directed credits, often at subsidized rates established by the government.	Differentiated requirements. No remuneration; one bank exempted from requirement on foreign exchange deposits.	Small amounts issued since 1994 by ministry of economy and finance at rates established by it.	None.
Uzbekistan	1995 law; independence in monetary and exchange rate policies; central bank credit to the government has to be approved by parliament.	Set by CBU.	At refinance rate.	Interbank credit auctions with CBU participation starting August 1993. All credit to banks through auctions and supplied by CBU.	Unified at 20 percent; no remuneration.	Treasury bill auctions since March 1996.	CBU certificates of deposits started in 1995.

Sources: IMF Staff Country Reports.

Figure 5.2. Interest Rates and Inflation
(In percent per month)

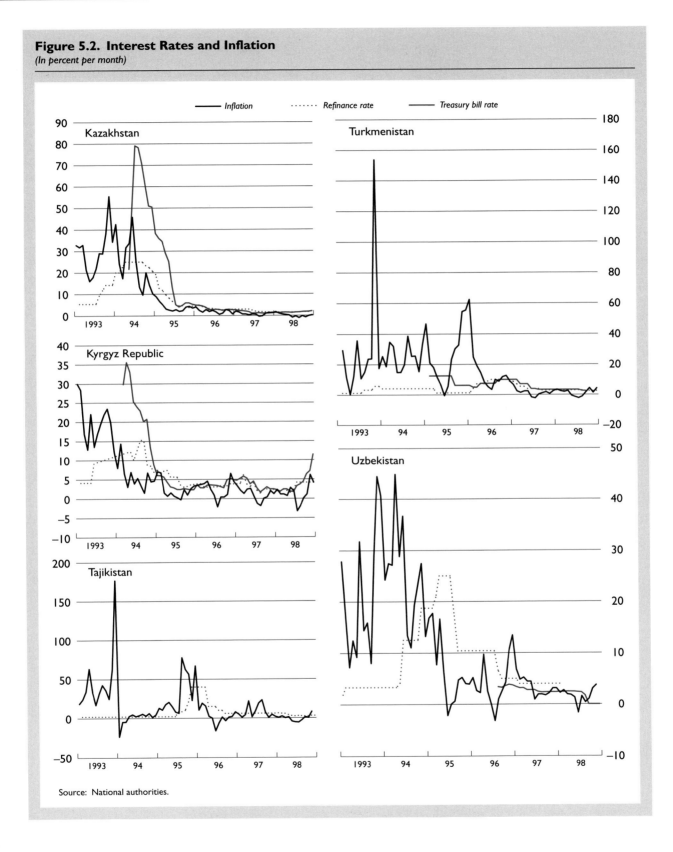

Source: National authorities.

was reversed in recent years). In these countries central bank credit was increasingly provided through credit auctions. By mid-1994, Kazakhstan and the Kyrgyz Republic had also removed all restrictions on banks' holdings of deposits of individuals. As a result, interest rates in Kazakhstan and the Kyrgyz Republic became largely determined by market forces, especially as the developing financial markets gradually took over the role of central bank financing. There were similar developments, although with some delay, in Uzbekistan. In Kazakhstan and the Kyrgyz Republic, real interest rates became positive by mid-1994 and in Uzbekistan by end-1994, although in the latter two countries there were short reversals to negative levels at end-1996 as monetary policy was eased (Figure 5.2, see previous page).[5] Real interest rates have gradually decreased from very high levels at the beginning of reforms. In Turkmenistan, a ceiling on bank credit interest rates was in force during most of 1995 and was reintroduced for agricultural credit in early-1998; direct credits at negative real rates set by the government continue to play an important role, and the yield on treasury bills is set by the ministry of economy and finance. In Tajikistan, commercial bank interest rates were not fully liberalized until May 1995, but since central bank financing continued to play an important role, interest rates were, in reality, set by the central bank in the credit auctions.

Bibliography

Begg, David K.H., 1996, "Monetary Policy in Central and Eastern Europe: Lessons After Half a Decade in Transition," IMF Working Paper 96/108 (Washington: International Monetary Fund).

Bredenkamp, Hugh, 1993, "Conducting Monetary and Credit Policy in Countries of the Former Soviet Union: Some Issues and Options," IMF Working Paper 93/23 (Washington: International Monetary Fund).

---

[5]The refinance rate is used as an indicator for all interest rates in the banking systems of these countries owing to the scarcity of reliable data on deposit and lending rates of banks. Although movements in banks' lending and deposit rates increasingly followed movements in the central bank refinance rate, banks' interest spreads remained high. For example, in Kazakhstan, the refinance rate was 35 percent a year in 1997, while the rate on short-term commercial bank credit was 45 percent and rates on deposits of households and legal entities ranged from 23–33 percent.

Coorey, Sharmini, Mauro Mecagni, and Erik Offerdal, 1996, "Disinflation in Transition Economies: The Role of Relative Price Adjustment," IMF Working Paper 96/138 (Washington: International Monetary Fund).

————, 1997, "Designing Disinflation Programs in Transition Economies: The Implications of Relative Price Adjustment," IMF Paper on Policy Analysis and Assessment 97/1 (Washington: International Monetary Fund).

De Broeck Mark, Paula De Masi, and Vincent Kohen, 1995, "Inflation Dynamics in Kazakhstan," IMF Working Paper 95/140 (Washington: International Monetary Fund).

de Melo, Martha, and Cevdet Denizer, 1997, "Monetary Policy During Transition: An Overview," World Bank Policy Research Working Paper No. 1706 (Washington).

Ghosh, Atish R., 1997, "Inflation in Transition Economies: How Much? and Why?" IMF Working Paper 97/80 (Washington: International Monetary Fund).

Granville, Brigitte, 1992, "Price and Currency Reform in Russia and the CIS," Post-Soviet Business Forum (London: Royal Institute of International Affairs).

Hernándes-Catá, Ernesto, 1993, "The Introduction of National Currencies in the Former Soviet Union: Options, Policy Requirements and Early Experience," in The Economics of New Currencies, report of a conference organized by the CEPR (London: Centre for Economic Policy Research).

International Monetary Fund, World Bank, Organization for Economic Cooperation and Development, European Bank for Reconstruction and Development, 1991, A Study of the Soviet Economy, Vols. 1 and 2 (Washington: International Monetary Fund).

Ize, Alain, 1996, "Capital Inflows in the Baltic Countries, Russia, and Other Countries of the Former Soviet Union: Monetary and Prudential Issues," IMF Working Paper 96/22 (Washington: International Monetary Fund).

Koen, Vincent, 1995, "Price Measurement and Mismeasurement in Central Asia," IMF Working Paper 95/82 (Washington: International Monetary Fund).

Sensenbrenner, Gabriel, and Vasudevan Sundararajan, 1994, "The Payments System and Its Effects on Monetary Operations: Recent Experience in the Russian Federation," IMF Working Paper 94/133 (Washington: International Monetary Fund).

Sundararajan, Vasudevan, Arne B. Petersen, and Gabriel Sensenbrenner, eds., 1997, Central Bank Reform in the Transition Economies (Washington: International Monetary Fund).

Wolf, Thomas A., Warren Coats, Daniel Citrin, and Adrienne Cheasty, 1994, Financial Relations Among Countries of the Former Soviet Union, IMF Economic Reviews No. 1 (Washington: International Monetary Fund).

VI   External Sector Policies

Jimmy McHugh and Emine Gürgen

Under the centralized planning system, the Central Asian states developed highly specialized and closely integrated economic relationships with the rest of the Soviet Union, notably characterized by a strong dependency on imports of energy, food, and consumer goods. During 1987–89, the region incurred trade deficits with the rest of the Soviet Union, averaging about 12 percent of GDP annually. The region's production structure was heavily oriented toward agriculture and mineral extraction, which left little room for growth of import-substituting industries. The export bases of the Central Asian states, therefore, lacked diversification, and import dependency was high, making these countries particularly vulnerable to adverse trade shocks. During the Soviet era, prices for energy and raw materials were far below world prices, so that the net importer countries in the region benefited from sizable trade subsidies. Turkmenistan—the only net exporter, whose primary export is natural gas—was an exception. Following independence, the Central Asian states (with the exception of Turkmenistan until 1997) continued to incur sizable and persistent external current account deficits (Table 6.1). Three main factors accounted for this. First, the agricultural, industrial, and household sectors inherited from the Soviet era were highly energy intensive. Second, the demand for investment goods to replace obsolete capital was high. Third, after years of repressed consumption, import demand for western consumer goods surged. Hence, imports from nontraditional markets grew rapidly, despite strenuous attempts (notably by Turkmenistan and Uzbekistan) to restrain imports, mostly through foreign exchange restrictions.

The newly independent Central Asian economies inherited state-controlled foreign trade systems from the Soviet era. Previously, foreign trade was subordinated to the requirements of the central plan, with price signals playing little role in the allocation of resources. State enterprises involved in foreign trade were confronted by a complex system of cross subsidies to offset the profits and losses arising from differences between foreign currency and domestic wholesale prices.[1] Exchange rates were administratively determined under a complex system of multiple currency practices. Export quotas were used to ensure compliance with bilateral trade agreements with countries outside of the Soviet Union. The management of foreign economic relations lacked transparency, with responsibility shared among several organizations, including the planning agency (Gosplan), the state foreign economic commission, the ministry of foreign economic relations, and a number of specialized foreign trade organizations. There was little opportunity or incentive for individual enterprises to engage in foreign trade.

Progress toward trade liberalization has varied across the Central Asian states. While the role of the state in foreign trade throughout the region has been significantly reduced, progress has been more pronounced in Kazakhstan, the Kyrgyz Republic, and Tajikistan, where highly restrictive state monopolies on foreign trade have been eliminated, licensing requirements relaxed, and significant tariff reforms initiated. Progress toward trade liberalization has been more gradual in Turkmenistan and Uzbekistan, where the state continues to play a dominant role, particularly in the foreign exchange market. The Central Asian states have benefited from the move to world trade. Exports have grown significantly, and the region has been broadly successful in diversifying markets. The movement toward world prices has, on the whole, benefited the region. A problem, however, has been the lack of an adequate payments system within the region, and with the region's traditional trading partners. Also, limited contract enforceability, continued reliance on barter trade (in some instances to settle debts), and limited currency convertibility have seriously inhibited the growth of intraregional trade.

External Sector Reforms

External sector reforms in the Central Asian states have covered five key areas: liberalization of foreign

---

[1]This system—known as the price equalization system—effectively isolated domestic prices from the effects of changes in world prices. For details see Wolf (1990).

Table 6.1. Current Account Balances

	1992	1993	1994	1995	1996	1997	1998 Prov.
			(In millions of U.S. dollars)				
Kazakhstan	−1,479	−438	−905	−516	−752	−912	−1,451
Kyrgyz Republic[1]	−98	−162	−124	−243	−425	−139	−285
Tajikistan	−53	−208	−170	−89	−76	−60	−133
Turkmenistan[2]	926	776	84	23	43	−580	−935
Uzbekistan	−236	−430	119	−21	−980	−584	−256
			(In percent of GDP)				
Kazakhstan	−51.4	−9.4	−8.6	−3.1	−3.6	−4.1	−5.6
Kyrgyz Republic[1]	−10.6	−16.4	−11.2	−16.3	−23.5	−7.9	−16.7
Tajikistan	−18.0	−30.7	−20.5	−14.6	−7.4	−5.5	−10.3
Turkmenistan[2]	54.7	20.1	1.8	1.3	2.1	−27.3	−36.2
Uzbekistan	−11.7	−7.8	2.1	−0.2	−7.2	−4.0	−1.8

Sources: IMF Staff Country Reports.
[1]Includes official and private transfers.
[2]Gas exports are recorded on an accrual basis. Nonpayment for gas exports are recorded as arrears in the capital account.

trade prices, reform of the trade system, market diversification, phasing out of barter trade, and currency reform.

Liberalization of Foreign Trade Prices

The Central Asian states followed Russia's lead in liberalizing foreign trade prices. The move to world prices in foreign trade had a mixed effect on the region. In the early years of independence, Turkmenistan and Uzbekistan enjoyed significant improvements in their terms of trade.[2] It proved relatively easy for Uzbekistan to shift exports of cotton and gold—traditionally supplied to the Soviet Union—to western markets. The move to world prices for energy within the BRO countries helped protect Turkmenistan's external position in the face of sharp output declines, including cutbacks in gas production. Diversifying gas export markets proved difficult, though. As of 1993, Turkmenistan was denied access to European markets through the regional gas pipeline network, so that its gas exports were confined to Ukraine and countries of the Caucuses. Hence, the benefits of the terms of trade improvement were substantially negated by sizable payments arrears by these trading partners for gas imports from Turkmenistan. By contrast, Kazakhstan and the Kyrgyz Republic experienced deteriorations in their

terms of trade, while Tajikistan encountered wide swings. As trade shifted to world prices, export and import prices surged at different intervals, generating sharp year-to-year fluctuations.

In 1993, exports of the Central Asian states to traditional markets—which at the time comprised two-thirds of exports—grew by 43 percent, largely reflecting the move toward world prices. While output declines that characterized the early years of transition were generally more muted in the Central Asian states, the effects of large output contractions in the BRO countries and disruptions to the payments system—coupled with the continued shift of trade to new markets—reduced the region's exports to traditional markets by 24 percent in 1994. Despite some subsequent recovery, the share of exports to traditional markets declined steadily during 1994–97. Kazakhstan, the Kyrgyz Republic, Tajikistan, and Uzbekistan continued to incur considerable trade deficits with the BRO countries (Figure 6.1). While Turkmenistan consistently recorded trade surpluses (on an accrual basis) until 1997, it accumulated claims of over $1.5 billion in unpaid exports against its traditional trading partners. As of 1997, the discontinuation of gas exports reversed Turkmenistan's trade balance with the BRO countries.

Reform of the Trade System

The Central Asian states inherited a foreign trade system that had partially undergone reform in the final years of the Soviet Union. After 1989, enter-

---

[2]This discussion is based on terms of trade data generated in the context of the IMF's World Economic Outlook exercise and suffers from certain weaknesses, as well as possible lack of comparability across countries.

Figure 6.1. Trade Balances
(In millions of U.S. dollars)

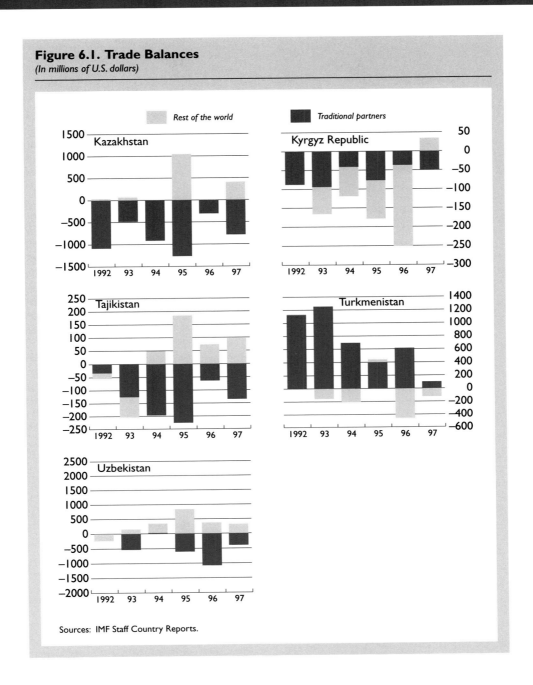

Sources: IMF Staff Country Reports.

prises could engage directly in foreign trade, rather than deal with state trading corporations. Also, enterprises were allowed to sell residual output after meeting production requirements of the state plan. To fulfill the production requirements, compulsory state orders and domestic price controls were initially maintained, triggering domestic shortages of some goods. To divert goods from export to domestic markets, explicit export taxes were levied in some instances and quantitative restrictions were applied.

The breakup of the Soviet Union accelerated the decentralization of foreign trade. The authority for trade relations was assumed by the ministries of foreign economic relations. The newly created state trading organizations quickly inherited many of the monopoly privileges enjoyed by their Soviet ancestors. Moreover, the legal framework inherited from the Soviet Union discouraged participation of the private sector in foreign trade. The absence of clearly defined property rights and the lack of legal means to enforce contracts made foreign trade

Box 6.1. Regional and International Trade Initiatives

The Central Asian states have taken a wide range of regional and international trade initiatives. All five have joined the Economic Cooperation Organization, which also includes Azerbaijan, Afghanistan, Pakistan, the Islamic Republic of Iran, and Turkey. The organization was set up to develop and improve the region's economic infrastructure and transportation system. Kazakhstan and the Kyrgyz Republic have joined a customs union with Belarus and the Russian Federation. Kazakhstan, the Kyrgyz Republic, Uzbekistan, and Tajikistan have formed the Central Asian Union (a single economic region) with the aim of improving payments arrangements and reducing import tariffs among member countries. All countries in the region have shown interest in becoming members of the World Trade Organization. In the case of Kazakhstan, the application to join the organization is at an advanced stage, while the Kyrgyz Republic signed a membership agreement in October 1998.

The European Union has granted all countries in the region access to the Generalized System of Preferences (GSP), which allows tariff reductions on manufactured goods and certain agricultural products and, in some cases, duty-free access to European Union markets. Most Favored Nation status was granted by the European Union under an agreement signed with the Soviet Union in 1989—the Trade and Commercial Economic Cooperation Agreement, which remains in force in the BRO countries. All countries of the region have gained MFN status with the United States and Japan. The U.S. has also granted GSP Status to Kazakhstan, the Kyrgyz Republic, and Uzbekistan. Japan is in the process of offering GSP status to all countries in the region.

renders, and terminating the requirement to register export contracts at the commodity exchange, although registration requirements were reintroduced for certain agricultural products in 1997. Tajikistan initially adopted a highly restrictive trade regime, although these restrictions were never fully enforced. During 1997–98, it introduced a wide-reaching program of reforms, establishing an open and liberal trade regime. Thus, the state order system, state monopoly rights, export licensing requirements, surrender requirements, and export duties were abolished. Nontariff restrictions on imports were also eliminated, and a low uniform import tariff was introduced.

Progress with trade reforms has been slower in Turkmenistan and Uzbekistan. In both countries, the state still exercises considerable influence over trade. Export surrenders and taxes are maintained. In Turkmenistan, all foreign trade—with the exception of gas, which is the responsibility of the ministry of oil and gas—is channeled through the state commodity exchange. In Uzbekistan, cotton, grain, and gold exports are channeled through the state sector, and the ministry of foreign economic relations continues to play an important role in trade agreements with nontraditional trading partners. Uzbekistan has made progress in shifting the burden of taxation away from exports toward imports by simplifying and lowering export taxes and introducing import tariffs. Both countries also engage in import substitution. Uzbekistan is aiming to become self-sufficient in energy and food. Thus, oil imports are discouraged, while exports of certain agricultural products—notably cereals, dairy products, and meat—are forbidden. Similarly, Turkmenistan is striving for self-sufficiency in wheat.

Market Diversification

As a whole, the Central Asian states succeeded in diversifying export markets. For the region, the share of exports to the BRO countries declined to 41 percent in 1997 from 68 percent in 1992 (see Table 6.2 and Figure 6.2). Similarly, the combined share of imports from traditional trading partners fell to 50 percent from 66 percent during the same period (Table 6.3 and Figure 6.2). The individual country experiences were varied; Uzbekistan and Turkmenistan experienced dramatic shifts in trade flows, while progress was less pronounced in Kazakhstan and the Kyrgyz Republic, and Tajikistan registered a rising share of trade (notably imports) with traditional partners.

Export growth to nontraditional markets has been impressive, with exports from Central Asian states to nontraditional markets more than doubling to $7.4 billion in 1997 from $2.4 billion in 1992. At

highly risky. Excessive licensing regulations and heavy actual taxation of exports, through complex systems of multiple currency practices and foreign exchange surrender requirements, impeded the growth of trade.

Progress with trade reforms among the Central Asian states varied considerably.[3] Kazakhstan and the Kyrgyz Republic quickly moved to abolish state monopoly privileges, unify exchange rates, and simplify the regulatory and fiscal frameworks governing international trade. During 1994–95, the Kyrgyz Republic dismantled the centralized system of trade arrangements. During 1995–96, Kazakhstan followed suit, by canceling monopoly rights of state trading organizations, eliminating nontariff trade restrictions, abolishing export sur-

---

[3]Regional and international trade initiatives by these countries are summarized in Box 6.1.

Table 6.2. Exports[1]
(In millions of U.S. dollars)

	1992	1993	1994	1995	1996	1997	1998 Prov.
Kazakhstan	3,562	4,769	3,285	5,164	6,292	6,769	5,748
Traditional partners	2,073	3,190	1,935	2,912	3,708	3,145	…
In percent	58.2	66.9	58.9	56.4	58.9	46.5	…
Rest of the world	1,489	1,579	1,350	2,252	2,584	3,624	…
In percent	41.8	33.1	41.1	43.6	41.1	53.5	…
Kyrgyz Republic	289	335	340	409	531	631	554
Traditional partners	216	223	223	269	394	346	272
In percent	74.9	66.5	65.5	65.8	74.2	54.9	49.1
Rest of the world	73	112	117	140	137	285	282
In percent	25.1	33.5	34.5	34.2	25.8	45.1	50.9
Tajikistan	185	456	559	839	770	746	651
Traditional partners	74	173	143	252	331	328	…
In percent	40.0	37.9	25.5	30.0	43.0	44.0	…
Rest of the world	111	283	417	587	439	418	…
In percent	60.0	62.1	74.5	70.0	57.0	56.0	…
Turkmenistan[2]	2,149	2,693	2,176	2,084	1,691	774	614
Traditional partners	1,934	2,370	1,669	1,422	1,142	397	…
In percent	90.0	88.0	76.7	68.2	67.5	51.3	…
Rest of the world	215	323	507	662	549	377	…
In percent	10.0	12.0	23.3	31.8	32.5	48.7	…
Uzbekistan	1,424	2,877	3,073	3,475	3,534	3,695	2,869
Traditional partners	869	1,440	1,684	1,186	643	961	…
In percent	61.0	50.1	54.8	34.1	18.2	26.0	…
Rest of the world	555	1,437	1,389	2,289	2,891	2,734	…
In percent	39.0	49.9	45.2	65.9	81.8	74.0	…
Total	7,608	11,130	9,432	11,971	12,818	12,615	10,433
Traditional partners	5,166	7,395	5,653	6,042	6,218	5,177	…
In percent	67.9	66.4	59.9	50.5	48.5	41.0	…
Rest of the world	2,441.9	3,734.7	3,779.7	5,929.2	6,600.2	7,437.6	…
In percent	32.1	33.6	40.1	49.5	51.5	59.0	…

Source: International Monetary Fund.

[1]Traditional markets refer to the BRO countries.

[2]Gas exports are presented on an accrual basis. Nonpayments for gas exports are recorded as arrears in the capital account. Transit charges are included in gas exports through 1995. As of 1996, all gas is exported f.o.b. at the Turkmenistan border.

the same time, export growth to traditional markets has stagnated, reflecting disruptions to the payments system, lack of convertibility of the new currencies coupled with significant foreign exchange shortages within the region, and depressed import demand for Central Asian products during a period of sharp output contraction in traditional trading partners.

Among the countries of the region, Uzbekistan made the most progress in diversifying export markets. The share of exports to the BRO countries declined to 26 percent in 1997 from 61 percent in 1992. Two main developments explained the shift. First, major Uzbek exports (cotton and gold) fetched higher prices in non-BRO countries markets. Second, neigh-

boring countries were unable to pay for Uzbek exports.[4] Meanwhile, imports from the BRO countries fell due to the government's policy of import substitution—notably the substitution of domestically produced gas for imported oil. Trading patterns changed more gradually in Kazakhstan, the Kyrgyz Republic, and Tajikistan. In Kazakhstan, the share of exports to the BRO countries declined steadily, to almost one-half in 1997 from close to two-thirds of total exports in 1992. This shift was partly accounted for

[4]The volume of gas exports in 1996 was one-half its level in 1995. Over the same period, cotton exports to BRO countries markets fell by two-thirds.

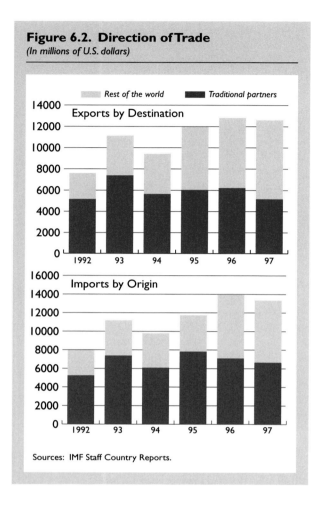

Figure 6.2. Direction of Trade
(In millions of U.S. dollars)

Sources: IMF Staff Country Reports.

year, nontraditional markets were the source of about half of Turkmenistan's imports.

Phasing Out of Barter Trade

In order to resolve payments difficulties, the Central Asian states resorted to barter trade, primarily through interstate bilateral trade agreements. Available information suggests that barter trade is important, particularly in Turkmenistan,[6] where large quantities of gas are exported through such arrangements, and in Tajikistan, where aluminum is also exported through similar arrangements. While barter has helped to maintain trade volumes, the goods traded have often been overvalued, of poor quality, and not necessarily in demand in the recipient country. Within the domestic economies, barter has created a noncash parallel market for goods. Moreover, enterprises receiving payments in the form of barter goods have often used surplus supplies to make payments on their outstanding debts. Barter trade may also have impeded the restructuring of domestic economies, since it is generally the older, less efficient industries that have been heavily involved in barter. In many cases, barter trade has permitted the production of goods that otherwise would not find a market. Valuation problems in barter trade have presented serious problems. The overvaluation of barter trade has distorted balance of payments statistics.

In recognition of these drawbacks, the Central Asian states have taken steps to discourage barter trade. Kazakhstan has passed legislation to prohibit barter trade, while Uzbekistan has issued a list of exports excluded from such trade. Turkmenistan has had some success in reducing the barter component on non-gas exports; since 1996, cotton, oil, and oil derivatives have been increasingly traded on a cash basis. Despite these initiatives, however, barter continues to be an important component of regional trade.

Currency Reform and Exchange Regimes

Initially the Central Asian states adopted the Russian ruble as their domestic currency, with each central bank maintaining a correspondent account in Moscow for interstate settlements. Monetary union was expected to minimize the disruption to foreign trade with traditional partners. However, the lack of convertibility of the ruble proved problematic and a

by greater access to trade finance that opened up new export markets, particularly in the European Union. The share of imports from the BRO countries declined by a similar amount. Trade between the Kyrgyz Republic and its traditional trading partners recovered, after five years of decline, mainly in response to a recovery in economic activity in the BRO countries. Despite some fluctuations, Tajikistan generally showed a more steady trade pattern, with traditional partners still accounting for over 40 percent of exports and about 60 percent of imports in 1997. Turkmenistan's gas exports were channeled entirely to BRO countries markets, as of 1993, while a significant portion of cotton and oil product exports were shifted to new markets,[5] raising the export share of the latter to almost 50 percent by 1997. In the same

---

[5]While the region's export markets have shifted, the composition of exports continues to be heavily dominated by those industries developed under centralized planning. Exports from the region continue to be concentrated in fuels, metals, and agricultural products, particularly cotton.

[6]Trade data by type of payment indicate that in 1996, 24 percent of Turkmenistan's exports were paid for in cash, 54 percent in barter goods and construction services, and the remainder was accounted for by the accumulation of arrears. In subsequent years, the cash component rose, as oil and cotton exports were increasingly paid for in cash.

Table 6.3. Imports[1]
(In millions of U.S. dollars)

	1992	1993	1994	1995	1996	1997	1998 Prov.
Kazakhstan	4,683	5,183	4,205	5,387	6,618	7,154	6,949
Traditional partners	3,160	3,675	2,851	4,181	4,018	3,935	...
In percent	67.5	70.9	67.8	77.6	60.7	55.0	...
Rest of the world	1,523	1,508	1,354	1,206	2,600	3,219	...
In percent	32.5	29.1	32.2	22.4	39.3	45.0	...
Kyrgyz Republic	377	501	459	588	783	646	705
Traditional partners	304	317	264	346	431	396	365
In percent	80.5	63.2	57.5	58.9	55.0	61.3	51.8
Rest of the world	73	185	195	242	352	250	340
In percent	19.5	36.8	42.5	41.1	45.0	38.7	48.2
Tajikistan	240	660	707	880	761	785	780
Traditional partners	107	298	339	478	395	463	...
In percent	44.8	45.2	47.9	54.3	51.9	59.0	...
Rest of the world	132	362	368	402	366	322	...
In percent	55.2	54.8	52.1	45.7	48.1	41.0	...
Turkmenistan	1,009	1,593	1,690	1,644	1,532	1,005	1,137
Traditional partners	807	1,115	973	1,023	528	500	...
In percent	80.0	70.0	57.6	62.2	34.5	49.7	...
Rest of the world	202	478	717	621	1,004	505	...
In percent	20.0	30.0	42.4	37.8	65.5	50.3	...
Uzbekistan	1,660	3,255	2,727	3,238	4,240	3,767	2,812
Traditional partners	869	1,975	1,657	1,794	1,723	1,356	...
In percent	52.4	60.7	60.8	55.4	40.6	36.0	...
Rest of the world	791	1,280	1,070	1,444	2,517	2,411	...
In percent	47.6	39.3	39.2	44.6	59.4	64.0	...
Total	7,969	11,192	9,788	11,737	13,934	13,357	12,488
Traditional partners	5,248	7,380	6,084	7,822	7,095	6,650	...
In percent	65.9	65.9	62.2	66.6	50.9	49.8	...
Rest of the world	2,721	3,813	3,704	3,915	6,839	6,707	...
In percent	34.1	34.1	37.8	33.4	49.1	50.2	...

Source: International Monetary Fund.
[1]Traditional markets refer to the BRO countries.

segmented system of payments developed, with trade being conducted in both rubles and hard currency. The ruble zone, moreover, precluded the pursuit of independent financial policies aimed at reducing domestic inflation. As discussed in Section V, the Central Asian states introduced their own currencies in succession during 1993–95. However, in many respects, the early experience with domestic currencies was disappointing. Inflation persisted, necessitating periodic nominal devaluation of exchange rates for considerable periods after currency reform. Highly distortionary multiple currency practices mostly remained in place (Box 6.2) and dollarization was prevalent. Moreover, the new currencies failed to strengthen the interstate payments system. Only more recently are these trends being checked and reversed.

As part of the move toward more flexible exchange rate arrangements, all Central Asian states introduced foreign exchange auctions. Some states progressed within a fairly short time from central bank to interbank auctions. Presently, in Kazakhstan, interbank auctions take place daily and foreign exchange futures are sold at the stock market. In the Kyrgyz Republic, foreign exchange auctions were abolished in mid-1998, shifting foreign exchange transactions and the determination of the official exchange rate to the interbank market. Trading of foreign exchange takes place in the interbank market, where the central bank intervenes as needed. In Turkmenistan, a preauction screening process still limits the availability of foreign exchange to importers, and the central bank essentially determines the exchange rate. Commercial banks participate in the auctions only on behalf of

Box 6.2. Multiple Exchange Rate Practices

Following the introduction of domestic currencies, the Central Asian states maintained complex multiple exchange rate systems, complemented by legislation that required exporters to repatriate export earnings and surrender a portion to either the government or the central bank. The ensuing multiple currency practices imposed an implicit tax on exports, while subsidizing imports, which benefited from a more appreciated exchange rate. The central banks, moreover, used the foreign exchange obtained from exporters to purchase domestic currency at a more depreciated rate, with the associated profits not always transferred to the government.

Multiple exchange rate practices also contributed to foreign exchange shortages by encouraging the undervaluation of exports and diverting proceeds away from official channels of conversion. This promoted the rationing of foreign exchange by central banks, which, in turn, fueled parallel market activity. The channeling of economic activity to the informal sector added to tax collection problems and left some transactions entirely outside the tax base. Overall, multiple exchange rate arrangements lacked transparency, distorted resource allocation, and eroded budgetary tax revenue.

More recently, most Central Asian states have moved toward more flexible, unified, and market-oriented exchange rate regimes. Kazakhstan and the Kyrgyz Republic have eliminated multiple currency practices and accepted Article VIII status in the IMF. In 1996, Tajikistan unified its exchange rate and abolished surrender requirements. Following earlier failed attempts, Turkmenistan unified its exchange rate in April 1998, although it continued to restrict access to foreign exchange and sustained surrender requirements. Moreover, a tightening of exchange controls as of end-1998 has once again resulted in divergent exchange rates. Uzbekistan continues to maintain multiple exchange rates and surrender requirements.

their (enterprise) customers. With the unification of the official (auction) and commercial bank rates in April 1998 at the level of the latter, the commercial bank and exchange bureaus rates became effectively tied to the auction rate, as they were not allowed to deviate by more than 3 percent from the auction rate. In late 1998, a shortage of foreign exchange, coupled with lax financial policies, resulted in the reemergence of a growing spread between the official and parallel markets rates, with the latter rising to more than twice the official rate. In Uzbekistan, the central bank also effectively controls supply and demand in the foreign exchange auctions, and hence the official exchange rate. In January 1997, the commercial bank market was formally split off with a separate ex-

change rate, which, until July 1998, was not allowed to deviate by more than 12 percent from the auction rate. The elimination of this requirement in July 1998 did not immediately result in a widening of the spread between the two rates, suggesting continued government interference through rationing and screening. Meanwhile, the widely used parallel market rate was almost four times as high as the official rate in late 1998.

As noted in Section V, in pursuing macroeconomic stabilization, the Central Asian states were confronted with the choice between fixing their exchange rates to serve as a nominal anchor or adopting a money-based stabilization program, which required observing monetary targets while maintaining exchange rate flexibility. Both options had benefits and costs. An exchange rate anchor would afford greater policy discipline, stabilize traded goods prices, and offer a more transparent signal of a counterinflationary commitment, enhancing credibility. However, real shocks—such as terms of trade shocks—could not be effectively absorbed. Failure to defend the exchange rate peg could carry significant costs in terms of lost international reserves and a weakening of counterinflationary credibility. A money-based approach would offer a remedy to real shocks through exchange rate adjustments, but monetary targeting could be difficult in the absence of stability in the demand for money. Under this approach, real shocks could lead to excessive volatility in both the exchange rate and domestic interest rates, with adverse consequences for output growth.

Reflecting these structural changes and uncertainty, following independence, the Central Asian states adopted, more or less, discretionary monetary frameworks that were, in essence, informal inflation targeting regimes. All countries adopted floating exchange rates, although the central banks frequently intervened to limit movements in the exchange rate (managed float), and some even, at times, adopted an informal peg. While all countries closely monitored the exchange rate, disinflation was ultimately achieved by bringing monetary expansion under control.

Currency Substitution

Anecdotal evidence throughout the region suggests that the introduction of domestic currencies was accompanied by widespread currency substitution, mainly as a hedge against inflation and exchange rate depreciation.[7] Distrust of the domestic

---

[7]For an econometric analysis of currency substitution in the Kyrgyz Republic, see Appendix I in Catsambas (1999). The

Table 6.4. Exchange Rates

	1993	1994	1995	1996	1997	1998 Prov.
	(Domestic currency per U.S. dollar; end-of-period)					
Kazakhstan	6	54	64	74	76	85
Kyrgyz Republic	8	11	11	17	17	29
Tajikistan[1]	1,247	3,550	294	328	748	977
Turkmenistan[2]	2	75	200	4,070	4,165	5,200
Uzbekistan[2]	1	25	36	55	80	110
	(Domestic currency per U.S. dollar; period average)					
Kazakhstan	3	38	61	68	76	79
Kyrgyz Republic	4	11	11	13	17	21
Tajikistan[1]	...	...	123	296	581	786
Turkmenistan[2]	2	36	1,402	3,258	4,143	4,890
Uzbekistan[2]	1	11	30	40	66	95

Sources: National authorities; and IMF staff estimates.
[1] Until 1994, Russian rubles; as of 1995, Tajik rubles.
[2] Official rate.

banking systems (because of restrictions on cash withdrawals and, more recently, episodes of banking crises), access of tax authorities to bank accounts, and foreign exchange controls also encouraged currency substitution. The latter contributed to macroeconomic difficulties by weakening monetary control, reducing tax revenue, and, more generally, complicating policy formulation. For example, where there was significant currency substitution, the expenditure-switching effects of a devaluation were limited because relative prices were determined mostly in the parallel market, where the exchange rate was already more depreciated. By reducing the parallel market spread, a devaluation acted as a powerful signaling device, indicating a possible shift in policies. Also, reductions in parallel market spreads encouraged reverse currency substitution.

The Central Asian states responded to currency substitution by legalizing foreign currency deposits, thereby reducing incentives for capital flight and channeling a large quantity of foreign exchange away from the informal economy. The simplification of exchange systems through the phasing out of multiple currency practices also helped reduce currency substitution by removing, or at least narrowing, the spreads between the parallel

analysis indicates that the interest rate differential and the depreciation of the exchange rate are significant determinants of currency substitution in the Kyrgyz Republic, and that policy measures—provided that they are sufficiently strong and implemented over an extended period—may have an important impact on the portfolio decisions of the private sector.

market and official exchange rates. International experience shows that only a credible and sustained counterinflationary stabilization program can effectively eliminate the incentives for holding foreign currency. As the stabilization programs under way in these countries firmly take hold, the conditions that breed currency substitution can be expected to disappear over time.

International Competitiveness

The broadest conventional measure of international competitiveness is the real exchange rate, which adjusts the nominal exchange rate by the ratio of domestic to foreign prices. A recent study by Halpern and Wyplosz (1996) points out that the real exchange rate in transition economies tends to follow a similar pattern. During the initial move to a market economy, the real exchange rate depreciates significantly; as market reforms are consolidated, it gradually appreciates. Possible explanatory factors are cited: economic restructuring, which leads to rapid productivity growth; abolition of price controls on nontradables, which raises the domestic price level and the real exchange rate; improvements in the quality of goods, which improves the terms of trade; widespread public sector reform, which shifts relative prices; and unsterilized capital inflows, which trigger nominal appreciations of the exchange rate. Thus, the real exchange rate appreciations observed may indicate an equilibrium adjustment to the process of transition, without necessarily having a negative impact on external competitiveness. Also,

Figure 6.3. Nominal and Real Exchange Rates[1]

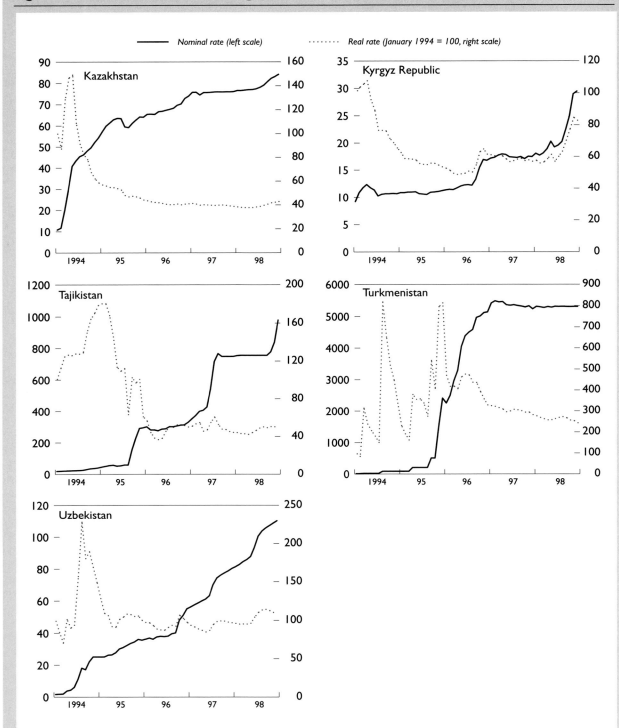

Source: International Monetary Fund.
[1]The nominal rate is expressed in domestic currency units per U.S. dollar; an increase indicates a depreciation. The real exchange rate index is calculated by adjusting the nominal exchange rate, expressed in domestic currency units per U.S. dollar, for the differential between domestic and U.S. inflation (CPI); an increase indicates a real depreciation.

Table 6.5. Gross Official Reserves

	1992	1993	1994	1995	1996	1997	1998 Prov.
			(In millions of U.S. dollars; end-of-period)				
Kazakhstan	83	541	907	1,194	1,980	2,244	1,967
Kyrgyz Republic	24	63	98	115	118	200	189
Tajikistan	0	2	1	4	14	30	65
Turkmenistan	0	818	927	1,170	1,172	1,285	1,379
Uzbekistan	82	1,031	1,341	1,867	1,901	1,167	1,168
			(In months of imports)				
Kazakhstan	0.2	1.3	2.6	2.7	3.1	3.2	3.0
Kyrgyz Republic	0.8	1.5	2.6	2.5	1.6	3.0	2.6
Tajikistan	0.0	0.0	0.0	0.1	0.2	0.6	1.3
Turkmenistan	0.0	6.2	6.6	8.5	9.2	15.3	14.6
Uzbekistan	0.6	3.8	5.9	6.9	5.4	3.7	5.0

Source: International Monetary Fund.

a strengthening of confidence in domestic currencies as reforms take hold encourages residents to keep a greater proportion of their wealth in domestic currency, further contributing to a real appreciation of the exchange rate.

Table 6.4 (see page 43) and Figure 6.3 (see page 44) give details of real and nominal exchange rate developments in the Central Asian states. The most notable feature is that the real exchange rate has exhibited a great deal of variability in these countries. This is largely explained by the high levels of inflation, both domestically and in the region's traditional trading partners. Moreover, the countries in the group appear to have generally followed the widespread transition experience of real exchange rate appreciations, following initial steep real depreciations, although the timing of the turning points has varied among countries. Considerable care needs to be taken in interpreting this data. First, barter trade—which is still prevalent in a number of these countries—is not directly affected by changes in the real exchange rate.[8] Second, the existence of multiple currency practices distorts the impact of changes in the real exchange rate. Third, average wages expressed in U.S. dollar terms are still low relative to wages outside of the region.

---

[8]Typically, barter trade is conducted through a series of bilateral agreements in which the goods are notionally priced in U.S. dollar terms. If the exchange rate vis-à-vis the U.S. dollar changes, barter imports and exports are revalued in domestic currency, while the dollar values of barter exports and imports are unaffected.

Management of International Reserves

At the outset of transition, the Central Asian states had negligible foreign exchange reserves, and the rapid accumulation of reserves became one of their primary objectives. Table 6.5 and Figure 6.4 provide details of movements in international reserves of the Central Asian states since independence. All countries have made considerable progress in accumulating reserves, although the level remains low in Tajikistan. Turkmenistan—given its particular vulnerability to external shocks because of the volatility of gas exports—has continued to maintain presidential control over international reserves, while all other countries in the group have placed reserves under central bank management. More work remains to be undertaken in the Central Asian states to further strengthen the management of foreign exchange reserves, notably to clearly elaborate guidelines and reporting procedures, diversify reserve asset holdings, and improve risk management.

Bibliography

Catsambas, Thanos, Johannes Mueller, Jens Dalsgaard, Joannes Mongardini, and Qingying Kong, 1999, *Kyrgyz Republic: Recent Economic Developments*, IMF Staff Country Report No. 99/31 (Washington: International Monetary Fund).

Citrin, Daniel A., and Ashok K. Lahiri, eds., 1995, *Policy Experiences and Issues in the Baltics, Russia, and Other Countries of the Former Soviet Union*, IMF

Figure 6.4. Gross Official Reserves

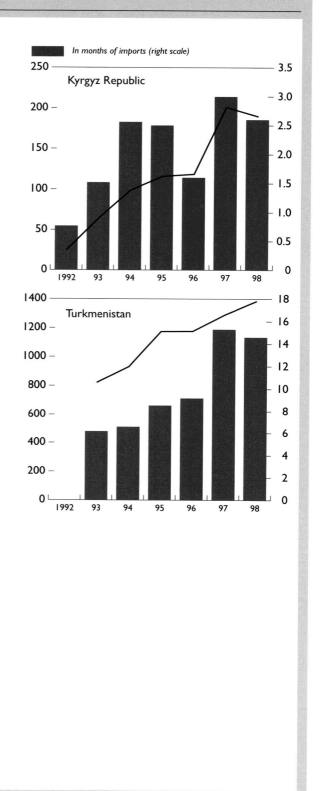

—— *In millions of U.S. dollars (left scale)*   ▬ *In months of imports (right scale)*

Sources: IMF Staff Country Reports.

Occasional Paper No. 133 (Washington: International Monetary Fund).

Halpern, Lázló, and Charles Wyplosz, 1996, "Equilibrium Exchange Rates in Transition Economies," IMF Working Paper 96/125 (Washington: International Monetary Fund).

International Monetary Fund, World Bank, Organization for Economic Cooperation and Development, European Bank for Reconstruction and Development, 1991, *A Study of the Soviet Economy*, Vol. 1 (Washington: International Monetary Fund).

Sahay, Ratna, and Carlos A. Végh, 1995, "Dollarization in Transition Economies: Evidence and Policy Implications," IMF Working Paper 95/96 (Washington: International Monetary Fund).

Tarr, David G., 1994, "Terms-of-Trade Effects of Moving to World Prices in Countries of the Former Soviet Union," *Journal of Comparative Economics*, Vol. 18, pp. 1–24.

Wolf, Thomas A., 1990, "Market-Oriented Reform of Foreign Trade in Planned Economies," IMF Working Paper 90/28 (Washington: International Monetary Fund).

Zettelmeyer, Jeromin, and Daniel A. Citrin, 1995, "Stabilization: Fixed Versus Flexible Exchange Rates," in *Policy Experiences and Issues in the Baltics, Russia, and Other Countries of the Former Soviet Union*, ed. by Daniel A. Citrin and Ashok K. Lahiri, IMF Occasional Paper No. 133 (Washington: International Monetary Fund).

VII   Capital Flows and External Debt

Jimmy McHugh

Total external debt of the Central Asian states grew almost sevenfold during 1992–98, reaching $10.5 billion by end-1998 (Table 7.1 and Figure 7.1). The growth in debt started from a nonexistent base; all of the Central Asian states had effectively accepted the "zero option" following independence, under which Russia took over both the foreign assets and liabilities of the countries of the former Soviet Union (Box 7.1). The subsequent accumulation of external debt in the region occurred in two distinct phases. During 1992–94, the breakdown of the traditional trade and payments systems within the BRO countries, the collapse of the ruble zone, and large current account deficits financed by credits from Russia all led to the rapid accumulation of intra-BRO countries claims. From 1994 onward, the Central Asian states increasingly experienced more conventional forms of capital inflows. In order to promote economic growth—especially in export-oriented industries such as oil, natural gas, agriculture, and metal extraction—all five states resorted to foreign borrowing. Initially, most of the loans received were from official bilateral and multilateral sources. More recently, private sector flows—primarily in the form of FDI and commercial bank loans—have gained importance in a number of the Central Asian states (notably in Kazakhstan).

During 1992–97, the external indebtedness of the region rose but, as a whole, remained moderate by international standards, both in terms of the size of the debt stock and the ability to service the debt. In 1997, the debt to GDP ratio and the debt service ratio in the region were, on average, 26 percent and 9 percent, respectively. The average debt service ratio in these countries is estimated to have risen sharply to 29 percent in 1998 (Table 7.2), reflecting a bunching of repayments, as well as a weakening in exports following the Russian crisis. As in the rest of the BRO countries, much of the borrowing that took place in the early years of independence financed current expenditure, including the settlement of arrears on wages and pensions, so that the returns that were needed to service the debt could not always be generated. If the recent rapid growth in external debt is sus-

tained and the funds are channeled toward unproductive uses, the region could develop a serious debt sustainability problem. In recognition of this, under successive reform programs, most of these countries have developed a keener awareness of the need to strengthen external debt management and to better prioritize the use of foreign resources. Also, the Central Asian states have made some progress in setting up debt management structures and restricting government guarantees, although more work remains, particularly in the areas of data collection and assignment of overall institutional responsibility for debt management.

Breakdown of the Trade and Payments System

The Central Asian states faced balance of payments difficulties following the move by Russia (their key source of imports) to using world prices in trade with the countries of the former Soviet Union. Initially, significant adjustment was delayed because the deficits were financed by Russia through so-called technical credits issued by the Central Bank of Russia in the form of correspondent accounts.[1] Based on changes in correspondent account balances during 1992, such transfers, received by the Central Asian states as a proportion of GDP, were estimated at about 42 percent for Tajikistan, 34 percent for Turkmenistan, 28 percent for Uzbekistan, 15 percent for Kazakhstan, and 11 percent for the Kyrgyz Republic.[2]

The Russian Federation became increasingly reluctant to continue financing the trade deficits of other countries of the former Soviet Union. In April 1993, it announced that the previous arrangements would be terminated, and that all future credits would be issued on the condition that all outstanding

---

[1]The newly independent states of the BRO countries abolished the old centralized interbranch payments system based on the State Bank of the U.S.S.R. (Gosbank), and introduced a new payments system based on a series of bilateral correspondent accounts held in each newly created central bank.

[2]International Monetary Fund (1994).

Table 7.1. Public External Debt

	1992	1993	1994	1995	1996	1997	1998 Prov.
			(In millions of U.S. dollars)				
Kazakhstan	1,244	1,848	2,717	3,428	3,889	4,601	3,986
Kyrgyz Republic	5	292	414	585	733	957	1,123
Tajikistan	217	509	760	817	868	1,180	1,261
Turkmenistan	0	168	418	550	667	1,356	1,743
Uzbekistan	62	1,039	1,107	1,782	2,331	2,545	2,376
Total	1,528	3,856	5,416	7,161	8,488	10,638	10,489
			(In percent of GDP)				
Kazakhstan	43.2	39.6	25.7	20.7	18.7	20.6	17.3
Kyrgyz Republic	0.6	23.8	37.4	36.4	41.5	54.1	65.8
Tajikistan	74.4	75.2	92.2	134.0	84.0	109.0	98.0
Turkmenistan	0.0	3.3	26.1	20.7	31.5	63.9	67.4
Uzbekistan	3.1	18.9	19.5	17.8	17.1	17.6	16.8
Weighted average	16.3	22.5	26.3	22.9	21.4	25.7	25.4

Source: International Monetary Fund.

balances on existing correspondent accounts be transformed into interest-bearing government debt. The Central Asian states (except Turkmenistan) agreed to this arrangement, thereby acquiring significant government debts owed to Russia.

In May 1993, the Central Bank of Russia stopped processing payments through the correspondent accounts, signaling an end to the ruble zone. The collapse of the ruble zone left the member states with a series of bilateral correspondent accounts, whose balances were subsequently frozen. Disputes arose regarding the valuation of these accounts, as the new domestic currencies fluctuated widely. Therefore, the exchange rates to be used in converting the outstanding balances became the subject of protracted negotiations among the parties concerned. Nonetheless, some progress was made in resolving these bilateral disputes. In March 1997, Uzbekistan reached an agreement with Russia over disputed correspondent account balances, with the final agreed amount exceeding $500 million. In October 1998, Kazakhstan concluded an agreement with Russia canceling all mutual claims up to 1998, including all state debts due to Russia arising from outstanding correspondent account balances pertaining to transactions during 1991–94, outstanding rent due to Kazakhstan for the use of the Baikonur space complex, and related ecological damages. Kazakhstan has also resolved its dispute on correspondent account balances with Georgia. The Kyrgyz Republic reached agreements with two of its main creditors, Kazakhstan and Uzbekistan. Turkmenistan recently resolved a

dispute with Russia involving correspondent account balances valued at over $100 million, but contested balances remain with some of the other countries in the region.

The accumulation of interenterprise arrears among the Central Asian states added to the external debt of these countries. While accurate data on arrears are unavailable, anecdotal evidence suggests that they were widespread. Many state enterprises, which could not sell their products and faced growing liquidity problems, continued production and accumulated payments arrears with other BRO countries enterprises. In some cases, importers obtained government guarantees on commercial credit agreements, as a precondition for supplying further inputs. In other cases, external trade-related debts were restructured into government-guaranteed debt.

Among the Central Asian states, Tajikistan suffered most from trade-related debt problems. Unlike the other countries in the group, Tajikistan chose to remain in the ruble zone after 1993 and continued to receive transfers from Russia. In order to avoid disruption to the delivery of industrial inputs, the government issued guarantees on commercial credits, which were often contracted with very short maturities and on unfavorable terms. In October 1995, the government announced that it would no longer guarantee debt arising from interenterprise arrears and would regard all such debt as private commercial debt. By 1996, Tajikistan's outstanding debt stock exceeded $860 million (84 percent of GDP) and its debt service obligations

Figure 7.1. Public External Debt¹

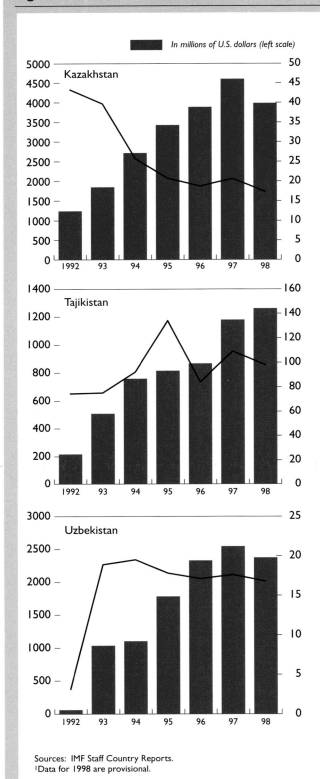
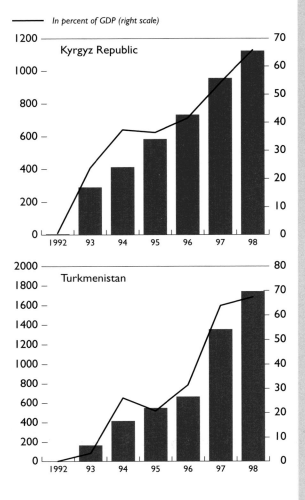

Sources: IMF Staff Country Reports.
¹Data for 1998 are provisional.

Box 7.1. External Debt of the Soviet Union

After the dissolution of the Soviet Union, it was unclear which countries would assume responsibility for the U.S.S.R.'s external debt commitments and claims. On October 28, 1991, Russia and the newly independent states signed a Memorandum of Understanding, under which signatories agreed to be jointly responsible for the debt, and to designate the Russian Bank for Foreign Economic Relations as the sole institution responsible for managing the outstanding obligations of the U.S.S.R.

On December 4, 1991, nine countries signed the Interstate Treaty, which indicated each country's responsibility for servicing U.S.S.R. debt on the basis of a number of key macroeconomic indicators. The signatories were also required to deposit foreign exchange reserves in the Russian Bank but the treaty was broken when only Russia met this requirement.

In April 1993, Russia proposed the Zero Option Agreement under which signatories would give up their claims on former Soviet assets in return for Russia taking responsibility for all outstanding debt of the U.S.S.R. All states except the Baltics accepted these terms, although some countries (Ukraine) have still not obtained parliamentary approval. The Baltic countries argued that they were legally never part of the U.S.S.R. and, therefore, the question of ownership of the former assets and liabilities of the Soviet Union did not arise.

reached 24 percent of GDP. Consequently, Tajikistan was unable to service most of its debts, and short-term financing to the country dried up. The National Bank of Tajikistan created a special debt service account for the government to meet current debt commitments and to service debt to those creditors who agreed to reschedule arrears. During 1996–97, Tajikistan reached agreements with Russia and Uzbekistan to reschedule their outstanding claims at concessional interest rates.[3] In a 1995 agreement, Kazakhstan rescheduled outstanding claims on Tajikistan.

By contrast, Turkmenistan accumulated large trade-related claims against Ukraine, Georgia, Azerbaijain, and Armenia, arising from the nonpayment by these countries for gas imports during 1992–95. Prior to 1996, the trade credits issued by Turkmenistan for its gas exports received government

guarantees from the importing countries. Although such guarantees were not sufficient to prevent the accumulation of arrears, the latter were subsequently rescheduled into government debt, with maturities of three to five years. As of end-1997, Turkmenistan held a stock of outstanding government-guaranteed claims totaling over $1 billion against these countries. Currently, Turkmenistan is receiving timely payments of interest and principal on this debt, with the exception of principal payments by Georgia, which is seeking a further rescheduling. As of January 1, 1996, Turkmenistan's gas exports are conducted on the basis of commercial transactions for which government guarantees are no longer granted. During 1996–97, private gas supply companies operating in the BRO countries (notably in Ukraine) accumulated a further $500 million in payments arrears to Turkmenistan, which have since been more than halved through repayments (although often in goods of questionable quality and price), as well as rescheduling.

Capital Inflows

During the widespread economic disruption caused by a breakdown of the trade and payments system after independence, the Central Asian states were considered to be highly risky by foreign private investors. With very low domestic savings, the region had to depend heavily on official bilateral and multilateral sources for financing new investment projects (Box 7.2). As the Central Asian states made significant progress toward macroeconomic stabilization, there was a marked increase in private capital flows in the form of commercial bank lending and foreign direct investment, notably into the traditional export-oriented, resource-based industries.

Under the system of government guarantees, often obtained from line ministries without central government clearance, state enterprises borrowed abroad heavily. Given their limited capability of generating foreign exchange revenue immediately, such loans became difficult to service and guarantees were often called in. For example, in 1994, the government of Kazakhstan was forced to assume external debt service equivalent to 0.6 percent of GDP on nonperforming government-guaranteed loans contracted by state enterprises, and subsequently canceled guarantees on $2.8 billion of undisbursed credits.[4]

Growth in capital flows was promoted by the easing of capital controls and reform of foreign in-

---

[3]The debt agreement with the Russian Federation was signed on October 16, 1996. The amount rescheduled was $288 million, with a three-year grace period, and amortization during 1998–2008. The agreement with Uzbekistan was signed on January 10, 1997 and provided for the rescheduling of debt in the amount of $200 million, with no grace period, and amortization during 1997–2003.

[4]International Monetary Fund (1995).

Table 7.2. Public External Debt Service

	1993	1994	1995	1996	1997	1998 Prov.
			(In millions of U.S. dollars)			
Kazakhstan	69	109	225	360	379	2,362
Kyrgyz Republic	5	7	73	48	38	43
Tajikistan	18	38	138	191	72	56
Turkmenistan	4	40	281	303	231	299
Uzbekistan	190	325	638	338	535	389
			(In percent of exports)			
Kazakhstan	1.4	3.3	4.0	5.2	5.5	38.0
Kyrgyz Republic	1.5	1.9	17.8	8.5	6.0	7.7
Tajikistan	4.0	6.9	17.7	24.8	9.7	8.6
Turkmenistan	0.2	1.8	13.5	17.9	29.8	48.7
Uzbekistan	6.6	10.6	16.8	8.6	13.2	12.0
Weighted average	2.8	5.6	9.8	7.7	9.4	28.6

Source: International Monetary Fund.

vestment laws (Table 7.3 and Box 7.3). The Kyrgyz Republic maintains the most liberal capital account regime (with full capital account convertibility) within the group. All of the other countries have maintained restrictions on capital account flows, primarily on the acquisition and sale of capital, money market instruments, and real estate, and on the purchase of foreign exchange by residents. In Kazakhstan, foreign investments have to be registered with the central bank. These restrictions have not unduly affected FDI flows.

Uzbekistan and Turkmenistan have the most restrictive capital account regimes. In Turkmenistan both inward and outward capital transfers are subject to central bank approval. FDI requires approval by the ministry of economy and finance and, for amounts above a specified limit, by the cabinet of ministers. Regarding outward transfers, usually only commercial banks are allowed to hold foreign deposits, financial instruments, and equity. In Uzbekistan, overseas portfolio investments in domestic assets are restricted.

Box 7.2. Investment and Savings in the Central Asian States

Under centralized planning, investment was undertaken within the context of an overall national plan directed from Moscow, with little regard to the efficient use of capital. Central planners focused on the accumulation rather than the quality of capital. Thus, there was a tendency to "overinvest" in projects with questionable economic value. Technical innovation was limited and the quality of new investment goods was low. The breakup of the Soviet Union accelerated the process of capital obsolescence. As trade barriers were lifted, state enterprises faced greater foreign competition, which exposed their technological weaknesses. Many of the traditional export-oriented industries such as oil, natural gas, and metals desperately needed to be reequipped in order to compete effectively in world markets. However, the region faced two major difficulties in raising funds from domestic sources to finance such investments.

First, financial markets within the region were underdeveloped, and their ability to attract domestic savings was limited. Financial services within the Soviet system were centralized, leaving a minimal financial infrastructure in the rest of the Union. Following independence, the financial sector in each state was subjected to excessive state intervention. Governments made extensive use of commercial banks to channel directed credits to ailing industries, which weakened bank balance sheets and eroded public confidence in the financial system. A second factor constraining domestic savings was the surge in consumer spending. Prior to the breakup of the Soviet Union, consumption was severely suppressed through rationing and shortages. After independence, there was a "catch-up" effect, as households and economic agents substituted consumption for savings. The changing pattern of consumer spending resulted in a significant increase in the marginal propensity to import from nontraditional markets.

Table 7.3. Capital Account Balances

	1992	1993	1994	1995	1996	1997	1998 Prov.
			(In millions of U.S. dollars)				
Kazakhstan	−105	1,172	1,194	1,160	1,367	1,442	930
Kyrgyz Republic	−3	73	158	249	347	259	212
Tajikistan	52	−29	−52	−36	−104	27	115
Turkmenistan[1]	−204	−551	−208	−51	55	764	893
Uzbekistan	224	858	−64	255	545	103	197
			(In percent of GDP)				
Kazakhstan	−3.6	25.1	11.3	7.0	6.6	6.5	4.2
Kyrgyz Republic	−0.4	5.9	14.3	16.6	19.0	14.7	12.4
Tajikistan	17.9	−31.0	−21.0	−6.0	−10.1	2.5	8.9
Turkmenistan[1]	−12.0	−10.9	−13.0	−1.9	2.6	33.2	34.5
Uzbekistan	−11.8	−7.8	2.1	−0.5	−7.9	0.7	1.4

Source: International Monetary Fund.

[1]Nonpayments for gas exports are recorded as arrears in the capital account, since gas exports are recorded on an accrual basis in the trade account.

Official Financing

Low-interest trade credits have constituted a significant proportion of bilateral capital flows, notably in Kazakhstan. By 1996, Kazakhstan had accumulated more than $850 million in such liabilities, owed mainly to Japan, Germany, Turkey, and other Organization of Economic Cooperation and Development countries. Turkmenistan also received large bilateral trade credits, primarily for imports of food and construction materials. A large proportion of total debt contracted was with Germany and the United States. As of mid-1998, about 67 percent of the Kyrgyz Republic's external debt was owed to multilateral creditors and 33 percent to bilateral creditors. Approximately two-thirds of debt was contracted on concessional terms (mostly World Bank loans). About 90 percent of Tajikistan's external debt is owed to official creditors—primarily Russia, Uzbekistan, and the European Union—but this mostly represents nonpayment of commercial credits on which government guarantees were called. In Uzbekistan, while debt to bilateral official creditors still represents almost one-half of the country's total debt stock, commercial bank lending has grown substantially since 1993.

Private Market Financing

Since 1995, there has been a marked increase in private sector flows into the region, with Kazakhstan being the most significant major recipient of such flows and the first country in the region to receive a sovereign credit rating. Subsequently, it has issued two sovereign Eurobonds, although one-third was postponed following the financial turmoil in Russia in 1998. The bond issues were considered by the Kazakh authorities to serve as a sovereign benchmark against which Kazakh corporations could borrow abroad.[5] Turkmenistan contracted a number of syndicated loans to finance infrastructure projects, the largest of which involved the rehabilitation of a major oil refinery in Turkmenbashi, coupled with the development of a number of satellite projects for the production of oil derivatives. It also borrowed heavily to finance aircraft purchases and to develop its airport. During 1996–97, Turkmenistan contracted short-term private loans to finance cotton production (partially collateralized by future cotton deliveries), which it rolled over in 1998. The Kyrgyz Republic is an example of a country in the region where private market financing was used in conjunction with multilateral financing and FDI; the $452 million Kumtor gold mine project was financed with a mix of private-sector loans and FDI supplied by the Canadian Cameco mining corporation.[6] During 1997–98, private financing was used to support the cotton harvest in Tajikistan. Despite these developments, private

[5]The first issue (1996) was for $200 million, with a three-year maturity and a spread of 350 basis points over the comparable U.S. Treasury bond. The second issue (1997) was for $350 million, with a five-year maturity and a spread of 245 basis points.

[6]The Kyrgyz government provided a one-third equity share to this company, as well as guarantees for the project and a 10-year tax holiday. During the initial years of the project (which started production in 1997) the bulk of the profits are to be used to repay foreign debt.

Box 7.3. Foreign Investment Laws in the Central Asian States

Kazakhstan

Reforms to encourage foreign investment have included the lifting of profitability controls, the establishment of a securities and exchange commission, and the adoption of a de-monopolization and privatization program. The 1997 Foreign Investment Law provides for tax holidays and customs exemptions for investments in priority sectors. Bilateral trade, investment, and avoidance of double taxation treaties signed with the U.S. guarantee nondiscriminatory treatment, hard currency repatriation rights, expropriation compensation, and the right to third-party international arbitration in the event of disputes. Foreign investors are permitted to engage in privatization initiatives. A number of special economic zones have been established, providing tax incentives to foreign investors.

Kyrgyz Republic

The Foreign Investment Law stipulates that the legal status and conditions recognized for foreign investors shall never be less favorable than those for domestic investors. The law provides for tax-exempt status for foreign investors for two to five years, depending on the sector of the economy. Full repatriation of profits is guaranteed. Six free economic zones were created in 1996. These zones permit virtually tax-free imports as businesses are partially or fully exempt from custom duties, excises, VAT, and income taxes. These zones have attracted very limited production, however, and were increasingly abused for the purpose of channeling imports through to avoid taxation. In late 1998, three zones were closed and regulations tightened. The government has created the Agency for Direct Foreign Investment, which registers and assists foreign investors.

Tajikistan

Tajikistan also offers significant tax incentives to foreign investors. Enterprises bringing in foreign capital of at least 30 percent are granted tax holidays on a sliding scale of between two and five years, depending on the amount of foreign capital. Foreign investors enjoy the same land lease and purchase rights as ordinary Tajik citizens, and may purchase natural resources. Mineral extraction requires a government license. There are no restrictions on the percentage of foreign ownership in a joint venture, and wholly owned foreign subsidiaries can be established. Foreign investors have equal access to government contracts.

Turkmenistan

A number of steps have been taken to encourage foreign investment. A series of laws were passed in 1993, which provided the legal framework for foreign investments, banking, taxation, and property rights. The government is working on the creation of a comprehensive commercial code. In 1993, seven free economic zones were created, which provide tax and production incentives to foreign investors. In early 1997, the Petroleum Law was passed, which allows production-sharing agreements in the oil and gas industries. Foreign investors are exempt from export surrender requirements.

Uzbekistan

The 1994 Law on Foreign Investment guarantees full repatriation of profits from foreign investment and access to foreign arbitration in the event of disputes. In 1994, joint ventures with more than 50 percent foreign participation were granted a five-year exemption from mandatory hard currency conversion requirements. In late 1996, a presidential decree granted tax breaks to foreign companies, subsidiaries, and joint ventures, which derive more than 60 percent of their total income from manufacturing and in which the foreign investment share of capital is not less than 30 percent.

---

capital flows into the region have generally been constrained in the absence of domestic financial markets.

Foreign Direct Investment

The Central Asian states encouraged foreign direct investment inflows, primarily by conducting far-reaching reforms of their foreign investment laws (see Box 7.3 and Table 7.4), which entailed, among other things, the issuance of guarantees on the unrestricted repatriation of investment and profits. They also reformed their domestic company laws to facilitate the formation of joint ventures with foreign investors, and Kazakhstan developed the institutional framework for its domestic equity market (Box 7.4). Available data

on FDI flows for the region suggest that, until the recent crisis in Russia, such flows were growing, particularly into Kazakhstan. Since 1992, Kazakhstan has received more than $5.7 billion in FDI, which accounted for about 76 percent of total direct investment flows to the region. A main advantage of FDI has been its close association with much-needed transfers of technology and managerial skills. The Kyrgyz Republic has received modest FDI flows, connected largely to the Kumtor gold mine project. Since independence, Turkmenistan has received more than $700 million in FDI, primarily in the oil sector. Cumulative foreign direct investment flows into Uzbekistan were of a similar magnitude during 1992–98. By contrast, Tajikistan has received very little FDI, despite its liberal foreign investment laws, with most investments

Table 7.4. Foreign Direct Investment

	1992	1993	1994	1995	1996	1997	1998 Prov.
			(In millions of U.S. dollars)				
Kazakhstan	100	473	635	964	1,137	1,320	1,132
Kyrgyz Republic	0	10	45	96	46	83	52
Tajikistan	0	9	12	20	25	30	12
Turkmenistan	11	79	103	233	129	108	62
Uzbekistan	9	48	73	100	84	167	226
Total	120	619	868	1,413	1,421	1,708	1,485
			(In percent of GDP)				
Kazakhstan	3.5	10.1	6.0	5.8	5.5	5.9	5.1
Kyrgyz Republic	0.0	0.8	4.1	6.4	2.5	4.7	3.1
Tajikistan	0.0	1.3	1.4	3.3	2.4	2.8	0.9
Turkmenistan	0.6	1.6	6.4	8.8	6.1	4.7	2.4
Uzbekistan	0.3	0.9	1.1	1.0	0.6	1.2	1.6

Sources: IMF Staff Country Reports.

concentrated in mining operations and textiles. Political turmoil and an unstable economic environment have reduced the attractiveness of the country for foreign investors.

External Debt Management

The Central Asian states had little prior experience in effectively managing and monitoring external debt because such activities were conducted centrally in the Soviet Union by the state bank for foreign economic relations (Vneshekonombank). A frequent consequence of this initial lack of debt-monitoring infrastructure in the newly independent states was the indiscriminate granting of government guarantees by line ministries, often without the knowledge of the government and an adequate assessment of the projects being financed. Also, countries tended to borrow under terms with short maturities, which often resulted in payments difficulties and the accumulation of arrears on debt service obligations.

To address these early problems, the Central Asian states increasingly focused on strengthening external debt management. In Kazakhstan, the finance ministry is responsible for external debt monitoring and repayments on all government-guaranteed loans. During 1995–96, a number of measures were taken to strengthen debt monitoring, including the introduction of the United Nations Conference on Trade and Development system for external debt management and creation of the Committee for the Utilization of Foreign Capital, which was given explicit responsibility for coordinating and managing government debt. Data deficiencies—particularly for loans contracted prior to 1994—have hampered efficient debt monitoring. In 1998, a decree was issued in Uzbekistan restricting the authority to grant government guarantees to the ministry of finance and the central bank, while in the Kyrgyz Republic debt management was strengthened by centralizing the authority to contract or guarantee external debt at the ministry of finance.

In Tajikistan and Turkmenistan, institutional responsibilities for external debt management remain less clearly delineated. Tajikistan has suffered from particularly weak debt management structures, which has contributed to an explosion of external indebtedness. More recently, the government has created, with technical assistance from the World Bank, a special debt management unit within the ministry of finance and has stipulated that all future government guarantees require the authorization of the minister of finance. Turkmenistan has complicated debt management arrangements. It is in the unique position, within the region, of being both a large external debtor and creditor, raising two very distinct debt management problems. The primary responsibility for managing government-guaranteed public debt rests with the state bank for foreign economic relations. The central bank manages its own portfolio of guaranteed loans. The situation is further complicated by the existence of a third source—the foreign exchange reserve fund, under the direct control of the President of Turkmenistan—which grants government guarantees. Debt owed to Turkmenistan

---

Box 7.4. Equity Markets in Kazakhstan

Kazakhstan has undertaken a number of important institutional reforms designed to strengthen and encourage the development of its domestic equity market. In 1996, the Kazakh National Securities Commission was created to oversee the development of securities markets. New requirements for the registration of brokers were introduced, minimum capital requirements for market participants were raised significantly, and the creation of a national association of broker dealers was encouraged. The securities commission drafted legislation providing a legal framework for issuing convertible bonds. In September 1997, a new stock market was established, replacing the three smaller markets for equities established after independence. Preliminary estimates suggest that the new stock market may have market capitalization as high as $8 billion (EBRD, 1997).

The Kazakh National Securities Commission envisages the development of a three-tiered domestic equity market. The first tier would consist of "blue chip" companies which would fulfill stringent listing requirements. The second tier would include companies on a pre-relisting board which would meet less stringent listing requirements. Finally, the equity market would provide over-the-counter trading facilities for unlisted companies. The development of the domestic equity market has been strengthened by the commitment of the Kazakh government to undertake a rapid and far-reaching program of privatization.

Kazakhstan has tried to link the development of securities markets to pension reforms, by establishing a number of private pension funds which are expected to provide the domestic market with liquidity. Available data suggest that the use of equity sources for private sector financing for investment projects has been limited, and largely restricted to Kazakhstan. There are early indications that foreign investors are showing interest in Kazakh equity. In 1997, a number of investment funds were created with the objective of investing in both listed and unlisted equities, and in convertible securities.

---

is primarily tracked by the ministry of oil and gas, although some debt monitoring is also undertaken by the central bank, and repayments are directed to both the foreign exchange reserve fund and the budget.

Improvements in debt management techniques in the Central Asian states have thus been limited essentially to developing the recording of debt flows and limiting the extent to which government guarantees are granted. Little progress has been made in developing risk management techniques. While data on currency composition of external debt are not readily available, the Central Asian states have borrowed heavily in two or three foreign currencies. They have large open positions, which exposes them to foreign currency risk. Sharp adverse swings in exchange rates could potentially create debt-servicing problems. Another important weakness of current debt management practices is the lack of a thorough evaluation of debt sustainability based on medium-term projections of the balance of payments, debt-servicing requirements, and future debt disbursements.

Bibliography

European Bank for Reconstruction and Development, 1997, *Transition Report* (London: EBRD).

International Monetary Fund, 1994, "Stabilization, Reform, and the Role of External Financing in the Countries in Transition," in *World Economic Outlook, May 1994*, World Economic and Financial Surveys (Washington).

———, 1995, "External Debt of the Baltic Countries, Russia, and Other Countries of the Former Soviet Union, and Russian Claims on Developing Countries," in *Official Financing for Developing Countries, December 1995*, World Economic and Financial Surveys (Washington).

Ize, Alain, 1996, "Capital Inflows in the Baltic Countries, Russia, and Other Countries of the Former Soviet Union: Monetary and Prudential Issues," IMF Working Paper 96/22 (Washington: International Monetary Fund).

Kapur, Ishan, and Emmanuel van der Mensbrugghe, 1997, "External Borrowing by the Baltics, Russia, and Other Countries of the Former Soviet Union: Developments and Policy Issues," IMF Working Paper 97/72 (Washington: International Monetary Fund).

Mongardini, Johannes, and Johannes Mueller, 1999, "Currency Substitution in the Kyrgyz Republic," in *Kyrgyz Republic: Recent Economic Developments*, ed. by Thanos Catsambas and others, IMF Staff Country Report No. 99/31 (Washington: International Monetary Fund).

European Bank for Reconstruction and Development, 1997, *Transition Report* (London: EBRD).

Wolf, Thomas A., Warren Coats, Daniel Citrin, and Adrienne Cheasty, 1994, *Financial Relations Among Countries of the Former Soviet Union*, IMF Economic Reviews No. 1 (Washington: International Monetary Fund).

VIII Structural Reforms

Jon Craig, Ivailo Izvorski, Harry Snoek, and Ron van Rooden

Achieving macroeconomic stabilization has been a key element of economic reform programs in transition countries, and many agree that sustained stabilization is essential for the resumption of economic growth. While stabilization appears to be a necessary condition for achieving growth, it is not a sufficient one. Another important condition for restoring sustained growth is structural reforms. In this regard, recent studies have shown that there is no shortcut to reforms; a comprehensive package combining progress in all areas, ranging from price and exchange liberalization to creating a market-oriented legal framework, is required.[1] Some of these reforms can be undertaken virtually overnight, such as price liberalization, but others take more time to develop and implement by their very nature, including securing property rights and establishing a rule of law. Still, developing institutions that create a market-friendly environment cannot be delayed for too long, as the institutional vacuum that may appear will create opportunities for rent seeking and corruption. This will foster the development of strong vested interests, which, in turn, will oppose free competition, undermine the application of a rule of law, and may bring the transition process to a halt.

This section describes the progress that has been made in the five Central Asian states in implementing a number of key structural reforms: price liberalization, enterprise reform, financial sector reforms, and fiscal reforms. Reform of exchange and trade regimes—an important component of structural reforms—was discussed in Section VI.

Price Liberalization

As described by Kornai (1994), one of the key changes that is needed in the transformation to a market economy is to force a move from a sellers' market to a buyers' market. This primarily requires price liberalization. When Russia launched its price liberalization program on January 2, 1992, the Cen-

tral Asian states had little choice but to follow. Kazakhstan and the Kyrgyz Republic implemented substantial price liberalization in the succeeding period and avoided significant policy reversals. With the exception of some monopoly products and utilities, Kazakhstan virtually completed its price liberalization by 1994 (when energy prices were freed) and eliminated most state orders. The Kyrgyz Republic initially kept subsidies on a small set of foodstuffs (primarily milk and bread), controlled the prices of monopoly products (including gas, electricity, and heat), and retained some agricultural state orders until 1993–94. In 1995 only nine monopoly prices were regulated by profit margin requirements, and by 1997 these were also mostly abolished.

Price reforms in Tajikistan, Turkmenistan, and Uzbekistan tended to be slower and more erratic. Tajikistan lifted price controls on 80 percent of all goods in 1992, only to reintroduce some control in 1993, and to resume price liberalization in 1995. By 1996, most prices had been liberalized, with the exception of utilities and transportation. Similarly, Uzbekistan liberalized most retail prices in 1992 but maintained a card system for price-controlled goods.[2] Some backtracking of the initial liberalization took place before price reform was resumed in 1994. By 1998, price controls still existed for utilities and transportation, and for a large number of monopoly products including most foodstuffs. State orders remain in effect for cotton and wheat. Turkmenistan kept over 400 goods and services subject to price controls until January 1995, when the number was reduced to 51. Following further liberalization in 1997, a number of goods and services[3] still remain under price controls; state orders are maintained for cotton and wheat.

All five countries in the group maintained administered prices for a number of natural monopoly

---

[1]See Havrylyshyn and others (forthcoming).

[2]Key consumer items (bread, flour, macaroni, vegetable oil, milk, meat, eggs, sugar, tea, and soap) as well as electricity, water, heating, and some other utilities were rationed at controlled prices through the card system.

[3]Most notably, flour, bread, milk, cottonseed oil, rice, and sugar; as well as heating, rent, transportation, telecommunications, gas, oil, and water.

services—notably electricity, water, heat, transportation, and telecommunications—that were priced below recovery cost. In all of the countries, prices for these services have been periodically adjusted closer to recovery-cost levels, but in most of them, prices still remain well below recovery-cost levels. Only Kazakhstan has made significant progress in this regard.

Enterprise Reform

A second key element of the transformation to a market economy is the enforcement of hard budget constraints on state enterprises via the elimination of various support mechanisms, such as budgetary subsidies, directed low-cost credits, tax exemptions and arrears, and interenterprise arrears. Together with price liberalization, this should provide incentives for the profit maximizing behavior of economic agents. Enterprise reform is needed to facilitate a reallocation of resources from old to new activities, via closures and bankruptcies, the creation of new enterprises, and restructuring within surviving firms.

Rehabilitation of State Enterprises

In general, the initial stage of the enterprise reform process—at times considered by Central Asian states' authorities as privatization rather than just a first step toward it—involved the setting up of state enterprises as independent units, that is, corporatization, during which enterprises were typically turned into joint stock companies, with more clearly defined owners and balance sheets. The second stage generally involved attempts to restructure state enterprises, either with a view toward their future privatization or liquidation, or to make them more efficient state-run entities in the case of natural monopolies. The leading reformers in Central Asia—Kazakhstan and the Kyrgyz Republic—have advanced the furthest in restructuring state enterprises. Uzbekistan has also made some progress; 130 enterprises have been declared bankrupt by the courts and 70 have been referred for restructuring, although there is no agency with responsibility for overseeing the restructuring process. Turkmenistan, on the other hand, has not yet started to deal substantively with the largest, loss-making state enterprises.

Kazakhstan has used various methods to deal with large loss-making, state-owned enterprises. Initially, to facilitate restructuring, enterprises were placed under management contracts with outside (including foreign) parties. By mid-1997, 12 contracts out of a total of 47 had resulted in a transfer of equity. Full buyouts were rare, however, and following increasing accusations of corruption and asset stripping, the authorities shifted emphasis to state-led restructuring under the State Property Committee and the Rehabilitation Bank, an agency set up with World Bank funding to restructure insolvent enterprises. The Rehabilitation Bank was intended to control all financial transactions of the state enterprises undergoing restructuring and to be their sole source of credit. By mid-1998, 26 out of 46 enterprises had either been liquidated or offered for sale. Meanwhile, the authorities have increased emphasis on case-by-case privatization. In the Kyrgyz Republic, a specialized agency—the Enterprise Reform and Resolution Agency—was created to deal with the restructuring of large, loss-making, state-owned enterprises. By 1995, the agency had completed diagnostic studies (sponsored by the World Bank) of 28 enterprises. During the evaluation phase, access to bank credits for these enterprises was cut off and some employees were put on administrative leave. Following audits, five enterprises were liquidated and four were removed from the program. The remaining enterprises were downsized, including through the divestiture of social assets, and restructured; the sale of these enterprises was almost complete by mid-1998. The rehabilitation of other public and private enterprises is to be pursued under an Asian Development Bank corporate governance adjustment operation.

Privatization of State Enterprises

Progress with privatization programs varied among the Central Asian states. Typically, the countries in the region designed their privatization programs in three stages. The first stage concentrated on the privatization of small-scale enterprises and housing, and was implemented by means of auction sales, employee buyouts, or outright donation to workers. The second stage entailed mass privatization of mostly medium-sized enterprises. The third, and final, stage involved case-by-case privatization of large-scale enterprises, including natural monopolies and infrastructure. The Kyrgyz Republic completed the privatization of small-scale enterprises (with fewer than 100 employees) during 1991–93, mostly through outright sales by its state property fund. Kazakhstan and Uzbekistan followed close behind, privatizing about 90 and 96 percent, respectively, of the targeted small enterprises. Turkmenistan has, thus far, privatized almost one-half of the 4,000 approved small state enterprises. Privatization gained momentum in Tajikistan during 1998 and over 1,100 small enterprises were privatized.

The methods and timing of the first privatization waves differed across countries. In Kazakhstan, beginning in 1991, approximately 10 percent of the assets of small enterprises were sold directly to managers and workers. In Uzbekistan, privatization began somewhat later in 1992, and was implemented through a variety of methods, such as employee/management takeovers and leasing arrangements. In Turkmenistan, the first stage started in 1993, with 80 percent of the small-scale enterprises sold transferred to employees (who were obliged to continue existing activities); the remainder was sold in cash auctions. In Tajikistan, until 1995, the privatization of small enterprises could be initiated only by the employees, thus constraining the process. With the exception of Turkmenistan, where housing reform has barely begun, almost all housing has been privatized in the Central Asian states.

By 1993, Kazakhstan and the Kyrgyz Republic were entering the second stage of their privatization programs, while Turkmenistan was still enacting its initial privatization law, and Tajikistan was in the midst of a civil war with all reform efforts put on hold. In Kazakhstan and the Kyrgyz Republic, a voucher scheme was the main vehicle for privatizing medium- and large-scale enterprises. All citizens received (tradable) vouchers that they used for direct purchases of shares in state enterprises or invested in licensed privatization funds. These privatization funds bid for shares in the state enterprises, which were then converted into joint stock companies. Employees typically received from 5 to 10 percent of the shares, while the funds could bid for 25 to 51 percent of the value of the company (the Kyrgyz Republic was at the lower end and Kazakhstan at the higher end of this range), and the remaining shares were sold in cash auctions. Voucher privatization has been completed in these two countries. The second stage proceeded somewhat differently in Uzbekistan and Tajikistan. In Uzbekistan each citizen could purchase 100 shares in one of several privatization investment funds, and each fund used these personal shares to purchase property from the government. The enterprises privatized in the second stage were first converted into joint stock companies and then sold either through coupon auctions or cash auctions. In Tajikistan the shares of the joint stock companies were either sold or transferred to the employees or remained in state hands. Turkmenistan is still largely at the preparatory phase of the second stage of its privatization program.

The third stage of privatization deals with large-scale enterprises, monopolies, or hard-to-sell enterprises. The disposal of this property involves initial corporatization, followed by case-by-case attempts to sell the enterprises. Some of these companies have considerable social assets, which complicates their sale. The third stage of privatization is proving to be a slow and difficult task within the region, although it is well under way in Kazakhstan. In the Kyrgyz Republic, the privatization program was relaunched in 1998, following a suspension in 1997 because of an investigation of past privatization practices and allegations of misconduct, but only a few enterpises were sold. Progress has also been slow in Uzbekistan, with only a few large enterprises privatized to date (Box 8.1). The privatization of medium- and large-scale enterprises has barely begun in Turkmenistan. While also a latecomer on the scene, Tajikistan made significant progress during 1998 in corporatizing and selling shares in medium- and large-scale enterprises. In early 1999, an international tender was announced for the privatization of 22 state-owned cotton ginneries, and the state cotton monopoly was liquidated.

Some progress has also been made in privatizing agriculture in the region. The present constitutions of the Central Asian states do not permit private land ownership. The state, therefore, remains the sole owner of all land and mineral resources, although it can allocate land to cooperative or private entities through leases of various lengths and grant right-of-use and tradable status. Initially, agricultural reform in the Central Asian states concentrated mainly on the transfer of land control from state farms to cooperative farms—by law, privatizing the land, but, in reality, maintaining old relationships, including through state orders and state monopolies of input and marketing services. In Kazakhstan, more than 80 percent of farmland has been privatized. Farm privatization has often led to cooperative structures, providing individual farmers with long-term leases and buyout options to the land. Execution of such options has been limited, however, because of unclear property rights, although leases can be transferred and inherited. In 1993, the Kyrgyz Republic started distributing long-term leases with transfer and inheritance rights, and now more than half of the arable land is leased on 99-year terms. In October 1998, an amendment to the constitution was approved, allowing private land ownership. The land code will be amended accordingly. Starting in 1991, arable land in Uzbekistan was transferred to cooperative farms and leased to individual farmers. The new land code of 1998, however, declared all land that cannot be traded or mortgaged to be state property. In Tajikistan, the revised land code of 1996 allows lifetime leases with transfer and inheritance rights, but the issuance of land titles has been slow. Land reform in Turkmenistan was initiated at end-1996. The program provides for an initial, free, two-year lease, with potential ownership rights afterward (but without the right to sell), contingent upon fulfillment of government-determined output targets for cotton and wheat. Registration of land titles has been very slow so far.

Box 8.1. Progress with Privatization of Nonfinancial State Enterprises

Kazakhstan

The small-scale enterprise privatization program was officially concluded in 1997 and attention then shifted to restructuring of the energy and heat sector, railways, and telecommunications enterprises, as well as to the continuation of the case-by-case privatization program, aimed at some of the largest state-owned enterprises. During 1997, a number of contracts were signed with foreign firms covering the sale and management of enterprises and of oil and gas fields. In 1998, the authorities committed themselves to the flotation of shares in four large "blue chip" enterprises and to sign contracts with lead managers on future flotation of an additional five "blue chip" companies, although these plans were delayed, partly because of the unfavorable international economic situation. They also undertook to review management practices to improve efficiency and transparency. All remaining medium-sized enterprises listed under the third-stage privatization are to be sold.

Kyrgyz Republic

By mid-1997, approximately two-thirds of the medium- to large-scale enterprises had been sold. A number of heavily indebted enterprises were also restructured with support from the World Bank with a view toward exploring whether they could ultimately be privatized. The privatization of larger enterprises outside the mass privatization program was halted in 1997, pending the outcome of an investigation on whether enterprises had been sold too cheaply. The investigation was completed in December 1997 and the privatization program was restored. The government has initiated a plan to transform state enterprises operating in the key areas of aviation, mining, gas, oil, and telecommunications into viable businesses that make regular tax payments and service their debts.

Uzbekistan

Initial privatization efforts concentrated mainly on housing and small-scale enterprises, where considerable progress was made. Several state enterprises have been transformed into joint stock companies. Despite the sale of 25–30 percent of shares of many of these companies to employees, the private sector does not hold a controlling share in most of them. Moreover, as long as the state retains at least 25 percent of the shares, it still has a controlling vote. Even when the state holds as little as 1 percent of the shares, a shareholder meeting cannot take a vote unless the state's representative is present. Beginning in 1996, minority stakes in 150 medium and large enterprises were sold to privatization investment funds in auctions. Individuals could participate by purchasing stakes in the privatization investment funds. Follow-up sales, however, have been delayed. The authorities are planning to privatize six large enterprises through international tenders.

Enforcement of Financial Discipline on State Enterprises

A key component of the enterprise reform process is the enforcement of financial discipline on state-owned enterprises. Progress toward subjecting state enterprises to hard budget constraints has been uneven. Kazakhstan and the Kyrgyz Republic had eliminated subsidized bank credits by 1995. In the Kyrgyz Republic, there is still budgetary lending to some enterprises at subsidized rates, although such lending is being phased out. The rest of the group has generally been less successful in these areas, as they continued to use central credit as a means of maintaining output and employment. In 1993–94, Uzbekistan replaced outright directed credits with central bank loans, channeled through the ministry of finance, primarily to the agricultural, mining, and steel sectors, but this was reversed in 1997. In mid-1993, the government guaranteed the extension of short-term credits at below 3 percent interest to finance enterprise wage increases in line with government wage adjustments. As of end-1996, directed credits to sectors other than agriculture had been mostly eliminated.

Turkmenistan terminated directed credits in early 1996, only to significantly resume them (on highly preferential terms) later in the year and during 1997–98, mainly to finance the agricultural sector. In Tajikistan, while directed credits were, in principle, prohibited by presidential decree in 1997, the central bank was instructed to continue issuing credits to state-owned enterprises.

Interenterprise arrears—often a substitute for bank or budgetary financing—were a serious problem in the Central Asian states. Attempts to periodically monetize such arrears fueled inflation and sent wrong signals to state enterprises about the government's intention to impose hard budget constraints. In 1994, Kazakhstan, undertook such an operation, substantially derailing its stabilization program. Likewise, the rapid credit expansion in Uzbekistan in 1993 largely reflected the monetization of arrears. Turkmenistan engaged in similar operations, although interenterprise arrears grew sharply, related partly to the nonpayment for gas exports. Bankruptcy procedures, another important component of enforcing financial discipline, are discussed in the next section.

Legal and Institutional Reforms

Legal and institutional reforms are an integral part of the transition to a market economy. Setting up a legal and institutional framework that guarantees and enforces property rights and safeguards private property is an important precondition for healthy private sector development. A major problem in the Central Asian states is the lack of experience with clearly defined property rights; legal systems in existence over the past 70 years precluded such rights. As important as the enforcement and guaranteeing of property rights, are the laws that assist economic agents in making and amending contracts. More broadly, the civil codes of the countries, dating back to Soviet times, need to be updated and transformed. With the exception of Kazakhstan, none of the Central Asian states have embarked on in-depth reform of their civil codes, a serious deficiency given the needs of the market system. Commercial disputes are also rarely settled in the courts, because of the general inexperience with commercial contracts.

Related to civil codes reform is the need for the development of corporate laws and the enforcement of bankruptcy laws. In the initial stages of economic reform, all of the countries passed bankruptcy laws that were aimed mainly at the liquidation of loss-making enterprises. Although these laws clearly defined liquidation procedures, they contained insufficient provisions governing the restructuring process. Kazakhstan, for example, applied its bankruptcy law (originally adopted in 1992) only after a major revision in 1994, allowing the restructuring of loss-making enterprises. Turkmenistan has never applied its bankruptcy law, while the Kyrgyz Republic's courts apply the law sporadically (only 14 out of 250 loss-making enterprises were closed and 25 were reorganized). However, the Kyrgyz State Property Fund now has plans to start bankruptcy proceedings against 400 enterprises in its portfolio, which is expected to help identify areas for improvement in the bankruptcy law and strengthen financial discipline. In Uzbekistan, the bankruptcy law has been applied more rigorously following a revision in 1996, which incorporated the concept of limited liability of the shareholders in joint stock companies; 130 of the 200 complaints filed with the courts have resulted in bankruptcies and the remainder have been referred for rehabilitation.

As of end-1997, the bankruptcy laws of the Central Asian states contained several identical basic elements (Table 8.1). Insolvency occurs when the debtor cannot meet its liabilities as they fall due, including tax obligations in the case of Uzbekistan (but not in the other countries).[4] All laws allow for

restructuring if the majority of creditors reach a binding agreement with the debtor. Liquidators are court appointed in all cases; in Tajikistan and Uzbekistan, creditors are also consulted before the appointment. Specialized courts have not been set up to apply the law, other than the arbitration courts in Tajikistan and Uzbekistan. As noted before, the law has not been applied in Turkmenistan, and only a small number of enterprises have been declared bankrupt in Tajikistan.

The Central Asian states have also passed a series of laws establishing a more level playing field for small and large enterprises and, in particular, laws safeguarding competition. In the Kyrgyz Republic, the 1994 Antimonopoly Law defines a monopoly as a company or a product with a domestic market share of 35 percent. The so-called natural monopolies (railways, communications, energy, gas, water and sewage, tobacco and alcohol) and the so-called permitted monopolies (civil aviation, oil, publishing, coal and gold mining) are subject to regulation, while the "temporary" monopolies[5] are monitored but not regulated.[6] The 1996 Antimonopoly Law in Uzbekistan considers a product or a firm a monopoly if its share is more than 65 percent, up from a 35 percent limit in the previous version of the law. The Antimonopoly Committee is charged with monitoring the prices of all enterprises, including those considered to be natural monopolies (gas, oil, communications, rail). Antimonopoly legislation is at an early stage of development in Tajikistan and Turkmenistan.

Financial Sector Reforms

Evolution and Reform of the Banking Systems

During the initial years of independence (1991–92), the banking systems of the five Central Asian states continued to be segmented and sector-oriented. The state was still—directly or indirectly through public enterprises—a major shareholder in most banks, which, as discussed in Section V, remained largely dependent on central bank financing. At the time of independence, the five states adopted their own banking laws, allowing universal banking. The number of commercial banks (which had already expanded from the five traditional ones[7] following banking sector reforms in the Soviet Union in 1987–88) continued to increase rapidly, especially

---

[4]See EBRD (1997), pp. 176–213.

[5]Monopolies that will be broken up by the restructuring and privatization of the associated enterprises.
[6]See EBRD (1997).
[7]The Promstroi, Agroprom, and Zhilsots Banks, the Savings Bank, and the Vneshekonom Bank.

Table 8.1. Bankruptcy Laws in the Central Asian States

	Status	Insolvency	Reorganization	Liquidator	Claims	Specialized Courts	Law Applied
Kazakhstan	Passed: 1992, revised in 1994 and 1997.	Debtor unable to meet liabilities falling due, or debtor's liabilities exceed its assets.	If majority of creditors reach a binding agreement with debtor.	Court appointed, no special qualifications needed, no government regulation.	Cost of liquidation, personal injury claims, and social security wages take priority.	None.	Yes.
Kyrgyz Republic	Passed: 1993, revised in 1997.	Debtor unable to meet liabilities as they fall due.	If majority of creditors reach a binding agreement with debtor.	Court appointed, no special qualifications needed, no government regulation.	Cost of liquidation, personal injury claims, and wages take priority.	None.	Yes, 14 out of 250 enterprises have been closed, 25 reorganized.
Tajikistan	Passed: 1992.	Debtor unable to meet liabilities or taxes; petition filed for payments 90 days overdue.	If two-thirds of creditors reach a binding agreement with debtor and court approves.	Chosen by creditors and approved by the court.	Liquidation expenses have higher seniority than all other claims. Unclear whether taxes, employee remuneration, and social security claims have higher priority.	Arbitration court.	Yes.
Turkmenistan	Passed: 1993, revised in 1997.	Debtor unable to meet liabilities as they fall due.	If majority of creditors reach a binding agreement with debtor.	Court appointed, no special qualifications needed, no government regulation.	Cost of liquidation, personal injury claims, and wages take priority.	None.	No.
Uzbekistan	Passed: 1994.	Debtor unable to meet liabilities or taxes; petition filed for payments 90 days overdue.	If two-thirds of creditors reach a binding agreement with debtor.	Court appointed, in consultation with creditors; no special qualifications needed.	Priority over all other claims, settled outside debtor's estate.	Economic and arbitration courts.	Yes, but infrequently.

in Kazakhstan (Box 8.2). Most new banks were established by state enterprises as a conduit for central bank credit. The structure of the banking systems, however, did not change very much. As most new banks were very small, the traditional banks (or their successors) continued to dominate the banking systems, accounting for about 75 percent of bank credit in Kazakhstan to 90 percent and more in Uzbekistan and Tajikistan at end-1992. All countries lifted the monopoly of the Savings Bank on household deposits during 1991–92, but continued to guarantee the deposits held with this bank, giving it a competitive advantage over other banks. Uzbekistan limited banks' holdings of household deposits to their capital for several years and, as a result, most household deposits remained with the Savings Bank.

Financial sector reform has constituted an important element of the reform programs of transition economies. Following the halt of transfers from the Soviet budget to finance enterprises, the role of the banks needed to change from mere administrators of transfers to the intermediaries between savers and investors, and to the allocators of scarce resources to the most efficient enterprises. In addition, banks were the conduit through which monetary policy—which became an active instrument—was transmitted. The efficiency and health of banks, however, was threatened by the impact of the stabilization and reform process, as borrowers had to adjust to ongoing changes, including sharply higher interest rates.

In the fastest reformers, Kazakhstan and the Kyrgyz Republic, banking sector reform was done in two stages.[8] In the first stage (1993–94), both countries began to eliminate small banks—many could not compete in an environment of higher interest rates and with a lack of directed credits—by raising minimum capital requirements. Banks unable to comply with the new requirements were closed. Given that the banks that were closed were small and generally held only deposits of their shareholders, this restructuring was implemented without much cost. In addition, licensing requirements were tightened and prudential regulations strengthened. At the same time, the government's share in commercial banks was gradually reduced.

In the second stage of reforms (1995–96),[9] bank supervision was further strengthened and the problems of the large banks were addressed. In 1994, banks were audited, revealing nonperforming debt

equivalent to 55 percent of total portfolios in Kazakhstan and 70–80 percent in the Kyrgyz Republic. These bad debts were mostly held by successors of the traditional specialized banks and related to government directed credits provided in earlier years. The importance of the larger banks often precluded their closure, although in the Kyrgyz Republic, the Elbank (formerly the Savings Bank) and the Agroprombank were closed. In general, banks were restructured through mergers, recapitalization by government or private sector funds, and transfer of a large portion of nonperforming debt to special debt-recovery agencies (Box 8.3). As part of their restructuring efforts, both countries introduced new central bank and banking laws, enhancing the powers of their central banks. Banking supervision regulations were brought closely in line with international standards,[10] while additional legislation was introduced to promote financial sector development.

The restructuring programs in Kazakhstan and the Kyrgyz Republic brought into the open the very high costs of the lack of proper banking procedures and supervision in the initial years of independence. In the Kyrgyz Republic, the total costs to the government of the reform were as high as 5 percent of GDP in 1996, or 31 percent of budget revenue, although these costs were financed mostly through long-term bond issues, and only the interest payments on them were immediately reflected in government expenditure. In Kazakhstan, nonperforming loans equal to 11 percent of GDP were transferred from the banks to special debt-recovery agencies.

Despite the progress made, the restructuring effort in these two countries is far from complete. In Kazakhstan, the share of nonperforming loans in total credit declined, but still exceeded 40 percent at end-1996. A number of large foreign banks brought much needed banking expertise to the country. However, the general skill level in many of the indigenous banks—the four largest of which still account for about one-half of total assets—remained low. Progress was faster in the Kyrgyz Republic. A large share of nonperforming debt was taken out of the banks and the recapitalization of the banks was stronger. By mid-1997, all banks complied with the prudential guidelines, and the share of nonperforming debt was reduced to 7 percent.

The other three Central Asian states progressed more slowly in the restructuring of their banking systems. Uzbekistan and Turkmenistan improved bank supervision, but in both countries little has been done to restructure the financial system, which

---

[8]For a detailed discussion of banking sector reforms in Kazakhstan, see Hoelscher (1998). The paper shows that although substantial reforms in the structure of Kazakhstan's financial system had been accomplished by the end of 1997, the banking system had not yet begun to play an active role in financial intermediation.

[9]In both countries, the banking sector restructuring was supported with World Bank assistance.

[10]However, Kazakhstan gave banks five years to comply with the new prudential regulations.

Box 8.2. Banking System Reform in the Central Asian States

Kazakhstan

The number of banks increased rapidly after the 1988 reforms to 204 by end-1993, although the banking system remained dominated by the traditional specialized banks. Banking system reform in the subsequent period reduced the number of banks to fewer than 100 by 1997 through mergers and closures. In December 1991, all banks were allowed to accept deposits from and lend to all sectors. Banking system reforms were initiated following adoption of a new banking law in 1993. In 1994, the specialized banks were reorganized, prudential regulations tightened, and noncomplying banks were merged or closed. The restructuring of the banking system was intensified during 1995–96, and the number of banks with state participation was reduced. Supported by new central bank and commercial bank laws, the National Bank of Kazakhstan further tightened prudential regulations, bringing them closer to international standards. Larger banks with a high share of bad debt were restructured and nonperforming loans transferred to two debt-recovery institutions. However, the share of nonperforming loans in the banking system, although declining, remained high. In 1996, the fourth largest bank was closed; in 1997, two other large banks, one private, were taken over by the government, merged, and recapitalized. The same bank was reprivatized in 1998. A program was also adopted, under which banks have to comply with all prudential regulations, including capital adequacy, over a five-year period.

The Kyrgyz Republic

The 1991 Banking Law allowed universal banking for all banks. Nevertheless, banks remained sector oriented and the four traditional specialized banks accounted for 85 percent of total loans by end-1992. Improved supervision of banks in 1993–94 revealed large financial problems and a high share of bad debts. Licensing was tightened, banks were prohibited from lending to enterprises with nonperforming loans, and intervention by the National Bank of the Kyrgyz Republic was stepped up, including placing banks under their temporary administration. In 1995, as part of a comprehensive financial restructuring program, two state banks were closed, and a debt restructuring agency was set up. Two other former specialized banks were downsized and recapitalized. In 1996, new central bank and banking laws were adopted, prudential regulations were brought in line with international practices, and preparations were started on legislation for the development of nonbank financial institutions. By mid-1998, almost all banks complied with the new prudential guidelines, and the share of bad debt in banks' portfolios declined dramatically compared to 1996.

Tajikistan

As in the other Central Asian states, five banks accounted for 90 percent of total bank credit and they still dominate the banking sector. Although the Law on Banks and Banking Activity of 1991 allowed universal banking, the banks remain sector oriented and most banks are directly or indirectly state owned. During 1996–97, banking supervision regulations were tightened and brought more in line with internationally accepted practices. Most banks fail to comply with the regulations, however, and major banks remain severely undercapitalized, and the share of nonperforming loans in banks' portfolios is estimated to be high. To tackle these problems, a number of initiatives were taken in mid-1998: a comprehensive bank restructuring program was initiated and diagnostic studies of the major banks were conducted; revised and simplified prudential regulations consistent with international standards were introduced, including loan classification and provisioning guidelines; and loan-loss provisions were made tax deductible.

Turkmenistan

The number of banks in Turkmenistan, most of which are directly or indirectly government owned, increased to 22 before declining to 15 in 1998 through mergers and closures. The banking system remains dominated by four traditional banks, which account for a major share of total bank credit. The bulk of banks' lending operations consists of channeling directed credits and foreign loans to designated state enterprises. A new banking law was adopted in November 1993. Bank supervision regulations were brought more in line with international standards in 1995, and even further in 1998, but compliance remains poor. Banks have not been audited by international auditors, but the share of nonperforming loans is believed to be large. At the end of 1998, a number of measures pertaining to the banking system were introduced, including mergers of several partially state-owned banks, reinforced sector concentration of banks, and the prohibition of state enterprises from holding accounts with private banks.

Uzbekistan

At end-1991, five traditional banks (out of a total of 21 banks) accounted for over 96 percent of all bank credit. The 1991 banking law allowed for universal banking, although banks could not accept deposits from households in excess of their capital until 1994. New banking and central bank laws were adopted in 1996, under which the central bank's powers to regulate banks were enhanced. In November 1996, loan classification and provisioning guidelines were issued and operations of 17 banks with excessive amounts of nonperforming debt were restricted, but implementation of the new regulations remains difficult. In 1998, the banking sector continued to be dominated by the state-owned National Bank of Uzbekistan, which accounts for 60 percent of all banking assets. The national bank and other state-owned banks extend directed credits to state-owned enterprises and enforce tax, trade, and wage regulations; enterprises without foreign participation are required to have only one bank account.

continues to be dominated by the traditional specialized banks. The banks have not been audited, and are thought to be largely insolvent, although there are no hard data to confirm this. In late 1998, Turkmenistan announced plans to merge some of the (partially) state-owned banks to further increase their specialization and to achieve greater government control. In Tajikistan, a wide-ranging banking reform program was initiated in 1998, including audits of the major banks by international accounting firms. While the number of small banks declined, the banking sector remains dominated by the traditional, specialized banks.

The experiences of Kazakhstan and the Kyrgyz Republic illustrate that it will take some time before banks in the region can play an important role in investment financing. Even in the two more rapidly reforming countries the role of the banking system continues to be limited. The currency to deposit ratios, although declining, remain high, indicating a reluctance on the part of the public to hold bank deposits. While the slow pace of development of the banking system may reflect, to some extent, a general lack of confidence in the new currencies of the countries, resulting in high velocities of broad money (see Section V), it also confirms that strengthening the public's trust in the banking system is likely to be a lengthy process.

Bank Supervision

Bank supervision was introduced in the Soviet Union with the advent of a two-tier banking system in the late 1980s. The 1991 Law on the State Bank of the Soviet Union required Gosbank to set up prudential regulations pertaining to minimum capital and capital-asset ratios, liquidity requirements, single borrower limits, maximum foreign exchange holdings, interest, and exchange rate risks. The licensing of banks was the responsibility of republican central banks (except for all-union banks). Following independence, the five Central Asian states followed the Gosbank model of bank supervision and the central banks became responsible for the licensing and supervision of banks. Because of a lack of experience, however, the issuance and enforcement of prudential regulations took several years.

As part of their financial sector reforms, Kazakhstan and the Kyrgyz Republic turned their attention to bank supervision in 1993. Initially, the main prudential regulation was a minimum capital requirement. In 1994, both countries initiated bank audits, while Kazakhstan further strengthened prudential regulations through introduction of a risk-weighted capital-asset ratio based on international standards. This was complemented by issuance of loan classification and provisioning guidelines in 1995. The Kyrgyz Re-

public also issued such guidelines in 1995 and brought prudential regulations up to international standards by early 1997 as part of the second phase of banking sector reforms. In both countries, the improvement in regulations was supported by a rapid expansion in the bank supervision departments of their central banks.

Bank supervision regulations in Turkmenistan developed along similar lines, although their enforcement has been much weaker and bank inspection needs improvement. Moreover, banks have not yet been audited. In early 1998, prudential regulations were further strengthened, including through an increase in the minimum capital adequacy requirement to the manat equivalent of one million U.S. dollars, and an increase in the capital adequacy requirement to 10 percent of risk-weighted assets. Uzbekistan and Tajikistan were relatively late in improving bank supervision. Uzbekistan introduced loan classification and provisioning guidelines, mandatory annual audits, and a strengthened off- and on-site supervision system in 1996. Prudential ratios fall short of internationally accepted levels, however, and loans are not yet classified adequately for sound risk management. Tajikistan tightened prudential regulations in 1995–96, but it was not until 1998 that they were brought up to international standards.

Accounting System

The accounting system that the Central Asian states inherited from the Soviet Union applied uniformly to the central and the commercial banks. The system included detailed accounts at the level of individual enterprises but lacked information needed for modern bank accounting. In addition, the unified system was oriented toward commercial banks and inappropriate for modern central banking. By 1997, Kazakhstan, the Kyrgyz Republic, and Uzbekistan adopted new charts of accounts, which are mandatory for all financial institutions; Tajikistan followed in January 1999. Turkmenistan still uses the traditional chart of accounts, although it introduced an updated version in March 1998 as an intermediate step toward introducing a new plan of accounts in line with international systems in 1999.

Payments System

Under the Soviet system, individuals made payments in cash, while enterprises transacted by means of payment orders or payment demand orders.[11]

---

[11]A payment order was issued by the debtor to its bank, requesting that payment be made to the creditor. A payment demand order was issued by the creditor to the bank of the debtor, requesting the bank to make the payment from the debtor's accounts.

Box 8.3. Method and Costs of Banking Sector Restructuring in the Kyrgyz Republic

By end-1995, total nonperforming loans in the four large specialized banks (Agroprom Bank, Elbank, Promstroi Bank, and AKB Kyrgyzstan Bank) amounted to som 1.5 billion, or about 9 percent of GDP, with performing assets of 3 percent. As a result, all four banks were largely insolvent, and survived only because of special terms on their liabilities to the National Bank of Kazakhstan and exemptions from prudential requirements.

The insolvency of these banks caused serious problems for the economy. The large share of nonperforming assets reduced banks' interest income, and the lack of confidence in the banks obstructed deposit mobilization. Banks thus lacked loanable funds, while they preferred investing in secure treasury bills over higher risk-bearing credit. Credit to enterprises increased only marginally, hampering investment and growth.

In 1996, the Kyrgyz Republic started a restructuring program for the four largest banks, supported by a loan from the World Bank of approximately $45 million. Under this program, the Agroprom Bank and the Elbank were closed and their recoverable loans—a total of som 816 million—were transferred to a debt resolution agency, which was charged with recovering these loans. The Agroprom Bank—which was replaced by a new interim rural credit system implemented with assistance from the World Bank—had few individual depositors, who were paid out from its liquid assets. The government assumed the debt of the Agroprom Bank to the national bank (consisting mainly of directed credits) of som 965 million by issuing 30-year securities to the national bank, with a 5 percent annual interest rate (the security could be paid off with receipts from the debt resolution agency). In addition, it paid som 84 million (part of which was advanced by the National Bank of Kazakhstan) to small depositors of the Elbank, while som 38 million from large depositors were transferred to a new savings and payments corporation.

The Promstroi and Kyrgyzstan Banks were recapitalized. The former raised new capital from its private shareholders (and the government issued som 20 million in securities in guarantee of credit to a government institution), reversing the negative net worth position to a positive one that exceeded the target of 8 percent of risk-weighted assets. The AKB Kyrgyzstan Bank was unable to raise new private capital, but, in recognition of the fact that a large share of its problems stemmed from directed credits, it received a som 127 million government security, bearing a 25 percent annual interest rate. As a result, by mid-1997, both banks complied with the National Bank of the Kyrgyz Republic's prudential regulations.

Under the monobank system, most enterprise payments were made through Gosbank accounts. Payment delays did not affect the latter's liquidity and it could easily advance the payment to creditors. In the initial years of transition, due to soft budget constraints and easy availability of low-cost credits, enterprises and banks lacked incentives to accelerate the clearing of payments, which could take months. When interest rates were raised, however, bank credit became less easily available, and as governments started to impose hard budget constraints on state enterprises, reform of the payment system became essential. All Central Asian states first centralized interenterprise payments in a clearing center within the central bank (1991–92). In the next phase, the countries started to automate the clearing process, with the objective of eliminating the large delays experienced under postal and manual clearing systems. This was supported by legislation to bring about particular changes; for example, in Kazakhstan the execution of payment orders was forbidden for a lack of funds, and Tajikistan imposed penalties in 1995 on banks that delayed settlements. By mid-1997, the interbank payment systems in Kazakhstan, the Kyrgyz Republic, Tajikistan, and Uzbekistan were fully or largely automated.

Fiscal Reforms

The major structural fiscal reforms pursued by the Central Asian states covered the budget process, including budget preparation and execution; expenditure prioritization and policies, including public investment plans and reform of subsidy, pension, health schemes, as well as other aspects of the social safety net system; tax policy and administration; and public debt management (see Section VII).

Reforming the Budget Process

Basic budget laws specifying the procedures and financial responsibilities of governments and the establishment of treasuries to manage and account for government financial flows are essential prerequisites to sound budgeting. Ideally, one might expect budget laws to precede the development of the treasury institutions. In practice, the legislative base has lagged behind in the Central Asian experience. Formal budget laws were not introduced in Kazakhstan and the Kyrgyz Republic until 1997. The Kyrgyz law has some interesting provisions, including establishment of a budget commission to review budget implementation, inclusion of externally financed project loans in the budget, and adoption of more detailed budget appropriation classifications for spending units. In Turkmenistan, a law on budgetary systems was approved in 1996, although a more comprehensive law on budget operations is now being drafted. A formal budget law is under consideration in Tajikistan.

There has been greater progress with establishing sound centralized treasuries. With the exception of Tajikistan and Uzbekistan, all countries in the region have operating treasuries to manage the execution of their budgets. Uzbekistan took the initial steps to establishing a treasury in 1996 but work on the drafting of the related legislation and staffing subsequently stopped. Tajikistan has recently made progress on establishing a treasury.

In particular, Kazakhstan has made steady progress since the formal establishment of its treasury in January 1994—a treasury single account has been established and the payment process has been taken over from the central bank; accounting of all borrowing and debt service payments has been placed directly under the treasury single account; and the accounting and budget frameworks and the chart of accounts have been redeveloped. In the Kyrgyz Republic, the treasury became fully operational in 1996 and was integrated into the budget execution process in 1997. All bank accounts operated by ministries and budget institutions, including extrabudgetary accounts, have been closed and their balances consolidated in the treasury single account maintained at the central bank. Control on spending by each ministry has been enhanced and monthly warrants are issued to ministries to limit spending to available resources, although problems with expenditure control resurfaced in 1998. In Turkmenistan, the treasury was established in 1994 to handle central and local government budget payments. Although the treasury has been operational since then, some improvements are needed, including the centralized recording of spending commitments and arrears. Communications with regional offices also require strengthening.

The coverage of the general government sector in the official fiscal statistics have varied widely among the five states. While most retain a republic or central government budget plus a local budget that is largely controlled and financed by the central government, there are, typically, a substantial number of extrabudgetary funds, including one or more social security funds, financing pensions, and other social expenditure. At the time of independence, a number of countries also maintained separate foreign exchange funds into which state-controlled export revenues flowed. All of the countries, except for Turkmenistan, have discontinued such funds. Recently, the task of compiling comprehensive fiscal data has been further complicated by the emergence of public investment programs, which are almost entirely foreign financed, often cover enterprise as well as general government activity, and may require collection of data from a wide range of sources.

Kazakhstan and the Kyrgyz Republic led the way in defining and measuring their general government sectors and producing relevant fiscal statistics. In Kazakhstan, the general government sector covers the central and local government budget sectors, as well as the operations of extrabudgetary funds and the quasi-fiscal activities of the banking system. Budget estimates are available on a comprehensive basis and the treasury data systems enable central and local government outcomes to be monitored regularly, with monthly fiscal outputs published with a lag of about four weeks. In the Kyrgyz Republic, the general government budget covers the central (republican) budget and the local governments, as well as the city of Bishkek budget. A number of independent extrabudgetary operations are outside this sector.[12] The treasury produces both an economic and functional classification for the budget sector on a quarterly basis, with a lag of six to eight weeks. Revenue and expenditure arrears are recorded, although there is no quantification of quasi-fiscal activities, which have historically been relatively small.

In Tajikistan, the general government consists of the central budget, the local government budgets, and two extrabudgetary funds—the social protection fund and the road fund.[13] A state foreign exchange fund also existed until it was abolished in mid-1995. Analysis of the general government sector suffers from the absence of timely and complete information on the two extrabudgetary funds. The budget presentations employed still follow the classifications of the former Soviet Union. The information on revenue and expenditure arrears is incomplete. There has been no quantification of quasi-fiscal activities, which the central bank has undertaken from time to time, typically by extending directed foreign exchange credits to state-owned enterprises. In Uzbekistan, there is a central and local budget and six extrabudgetary funds.[14] The so-called hard currency budget was abolished and consolidated into the central government budget in 1996. Data for the state budget and extrabudgetary

---

[12]The following extrabudgetary funds existed in the Kyrgyz Republic through 1998: pension fund, social insurance fund (providing mainly health-related benefits), employment fund (providing unemployment benefits), state property fund (managing the privatization program), medical insurance fund, agricultural development fund, industrial enterprise support fund, and housing fund. The state property fund is included in the general government budget as of 1999.

[13]The social protection fund was established in 1996 as an amalgam of the pension fund, the employment fund, and the social insurance fund.

[14]The employment fund, fund for replenishment of mineral resources and raw materials, road fund, Uzgosfund, social insurance fund, and fund for the Trade Union Federation Council.

funds are compiled each month, with a delay of about three weeks. Financing data is often inadequately specified and mixed with "above the line" items. Information on revenue and expenditure arrears is incomplete. The central bank also undertakes quasi-fiscal operations that, to date, have not been quantified. The privatization and business funds are financed by revenues from privatization operations; the funds collected are lent at preferential rates to newly created private firms and privatized enterprises. Turkmenistan's budget coverage is seriously deficient, with less than 50 percent of general government activity estimated to pass through the formal budget. One of the difficulties of interpreting the fiscal accounts is the often overlapping accounting of public enterprise and general government operations. The proceeds of public enterprises are often used to fund activities that would normally be funded by taxes. In an attempt to improve the budget coverage, the authorities now include estimates of the total revenues and expenditures of the four major extrabudgetary funds—the oil and gas development fund, the agriculture development fund, the transportation and communication fund, and the health fund—as well as the recurrent and investment expenditures of so-called self-financing ministries and enterprises in the consumer goods and power industry sectors. This is done for monitoring purposes only, though, with no treasury control over the funds' transactions.

Most Central Asian states have started to adapt the budget presentations inherited from the former Soviet Union to international standards, although much work remains to be done in this area. Moreover, while revenue and expenditure data for budget operations are often available within a standard *Government Finance Statistics* framework, information on financing operations and public debt is typically still deficient. More work is also required in some countries to document revenue and expenditure arrears and quasi-fiscal activities. Again, Kazakhstan has taken the lead, with the 1997 budget sector accounts employing *Government Finance Statistics* classifications. In the Kyrgyz Republic, considerable progress has been made in budget presentation within the budget sector itself, with monthly data now published in both economic and functional classifications, although classification problems still exist. Data on revenue and expenditure arrears are also available. Uzbekistan and Turkmenistan do not prepare their budgets according to internationally accepted standards, although work is under way to rectify this.

Expenditure Prioritization and Reforms

Public expenditure reforms in the Central Asian states have focused on strengthening spending in so-cial areas, notably health and education; phasing out subsidies; streamlining and more closely targeting the social safety net systems; reforming the pension systems; establishing means of providing unemployment benefits; and developing public investment programs.

The need to maintain basic health and education spending in real terms has received increased attention in recent years and specific programs are being developed to achieve this goal. In the Kyrgyz Republic, for example, education services are to be, at least, maintained in real terms and emphasis is placed on preserving high enrollment rates for primary and secondary education by, among other things, switching funding mechanisms from teacher- to pupil-based grants. In this regard, however, it should be kept in mind that quantity does not guarantee quality. Therefore, in the provision of education and health services, efforts are also being directed toward improving efficiency. In Kazakhstan, the authorities intend to introduce copayments on higher-level services and to consolidate underutilized facilities, while shifting spending priorities toward primary and preventive medicine.

Attention is also being given to improved funding mechanisms for health care. Kazakhstan established a new compulsory medical insurance fund in 1996, funded from local budget transfers and 10 percent of the payroll tax (formerly paid into the social insurance fund), to provide a basic package of health services. The Kyrgyz Republic established a medical insurance fund in 1997, that imposes compulsory levies on individuals to fund a guaranteed basic package of services. Turkmenistan has also established a voluntary medical insurance scheme that, at this stage, is used to subsidize the differential between pharmaceutical goods' prices and the level of budget support. Medical treatment and hospital care formally remain free and available to all, although, in practice, free public service is limited and patients must seek private services.

All the Central Asian states have social safety net systems inherited from the Soviet Union. Benefits under these systems have been too costly relative to available domestic resources, as the benefits apply to the population at large rather than to its poorest segments. Reforms have started to streamline the social safety net systems. Notably, progress has been made in replacing across-the-board subsidies and price controls with assistance targeted to the most vulnerable groups. Kazakhstan largely removed subsidies for food, housing, transport, and other items in October 1994. Subsidies were replaced by targeted cash payments and further efforts are under way to improve the benchmarks for the social benefits payment system. The Kyrgyz Republic followed closely behind. A unified cash benefit was introduced in January 1995 to replace generalized subsidies for bread, as well as various child and other allowances, with about a fourth of the population benefiting. The authorities have recently set a goal of ensuring that the most vulnerable groups receive, at least, 60 percent of the benefits provided. A wide range of subsidies were removed in Uzbekistan during 1993–94,[15] while central heating and public transport subsidies were abolished in 1996. Some services, including municipal services, continue to be subsidized, although at lower rates. Still, many price controls, including for most foodstuffs, remain in effect, with price levels below cost recovery. Efforts are under way to improve the targeting of generalized family allowances. Most food subsidies were removed in Turkmenistan in the period up until 1996. Relatively small subsides for bread and public transport remain, but are largely funded by state enterprises via cross-subsidization of products. Substantial general subsidies remain for gas, electricity, and water. Tajikistan replaced its general bread subsidy with targeted cash compensation payments to families in 1996, while simultaneously reducing subsidies for electricity and irrigation. The overall program, however, remained relatively unfocused, with substantial subsidies remaining for transport, housing, and utilities.

As shown in Table 8.2 public pension expenditures remain large relative to GDP in most of the Central Asian states.[16] They are often funded by high payroll contributions by employers (with employees bearing a relatively small burden), and are often paid with delays. Although pensions are usually based on earnings, most schemes involve some redistributive element, with higher income earners implicitly subsidizing lower earners. There is often a minimum social pension available to those whose work record is insufficient to support an earnings-based pension. Despite the fiscal burden imposed on enterprises, the pension systems have become a crude safety net measure, providing a limited benefit to large sections of the population. In addition to revenue problems, which have contributed to severe pension arrears in several countries, as the population ages, generous early retirement provisions can be expected to raise the ratio of beneficiaries beyond that which can be sustained by contributors.[17] Given these difficulties, all countries in the region have been turning their attention to pension reform. Most

countries have expressed interest in a multipillar scheme involving a minimum public pension available on a universal basis, regardless of work record; a compulsory, fully funded contributions element; and, in some cases, voluntary contributions which may be used to increase the base pensions.

Kazakhstan has led the way in this area, aided by the World Bank and the Asian Development Bank. At the beginning of 1998, Kazakhstan put into effect a pension reform program to transform the public pension system into a fully funded system. The existing pay-as-you-go public pension system was transformed into a defined contribution-funded system of individual pension accumulation accounts, coupled with a minimum pension guarantee by the state. Under the new system, all workers are required to save 10 percent of their earnings in accumulation funds.[18] Investment of the assets of these funds is undertaken by a licensed asset management company. Retirees under the pay-as-you-go scheme and individuals unable to accumulate sufficient private funds are protected by a minimum pension guarantee, indexed to annual inflation. The retirement age is to gradually increase for both men and women. The Kyrgyz Republic developed a similar program in 1998, with World Bank assistance. The current pay-as-you-go system, which has become unsustainable, will be adapted to an annuity-like system based on crediting payroll contributions to individual pension accounts. Benefits will be determined on the basis of an individual's contributions, while granting an appropriate minimum pension. Both the retirement age and the minimum requirement for years of service to qualify for full benefits will be increased gradually. A similar approach is to be followed by Tajikistan. The age of pension eligibility is to be raised gradually, early retirement provisions tightened, and greater scrutiny given to pension increases to ensure that they are affordable. During 1999, the government plans to establish individual retirement accounts, also with technical assistance from the World Bank. In Turkmenistan and Uzbekistan, plans for pension reform are less advanced, although work is under way in Turkmenistan toward introducing a self-financing pension scheme. In Uzbekistan, the immediate focus has been mostly on stabilizing pension fund finances by collecting contribution arrears and reducing the number of pensioners receiving a full pension.

The need for payment of unemployment benefits has not been widely acknowledged in Central Asia, partly because of a reluctance to concede the break-

---

[15]Including subsidies on bread, flour, rice, eggs, meat, milk, sugar, tea, and some nonfood items.

[16]See de Castello Branco (1998) for a more detailed description.

[17]At end-1996, all the countries in question had retirement ages of 60 years for men and 55 years for women.

[18]At end-1998, there were 13 accumulation funds, of which one is state owned. Workers are free to choose among these funds.

Table 8.2. Public Pension Expenditures
(In percent of GDP)

	1992	1993	1994	1995	1996
Kazakhstan	...	4.4	3.8	4.7	5.3
Kyrgyz Republic	...	...	5.2	7.5	7.7
Russia	6.9	6.1	6.1	4.6	4.5
Tajikistan	7.0	6.9	3.9	2.5	3.0
Turkmenistan	...	...	1.7	1.7	2.3
Uzbekistan	8.4	10.0	5.7	5.3	6.4

Source: de Castello Branco (1998).

down of the Soviet system of lifetime guaranteed employment. Generally, employment fund expenditures are very low and cover mainly training expenditures and some very limited unemployment benefits, financed by a 2 percent payroll tax.

Countries have started to adapt their systems to deal with the unemployment problem. In Kazakhstan, for example, the payroll contributions to the employment fund have traditionally run at 2 percent of payrolls but the workforce coverage was limited. From the beginning of 1996, the standard contributions were extended to all sectors and, as of January 1997, previously exempted budgetary organizations are required to contribute 1 percent of payrolls to the employment fund. The benefit levels will also be improved, with the replacement rate (the ratio of the average unemployment benefit to average wages) expected to almost double to 30 percent.

Historically, the planning mechanisms in place in the Central Asian states placed a heavy emphasis on public investment, much of which, however, failed to achieve lasting benefits for the economy. As financial constraints have reduced essential maintenance expenditures, there has been a substantial overall decline in the public infrastructure of the Central Asian states. The World Bank, in cooperation with other international agencies, has assisted these countries in formulating and implementing coordinated public investment programs, focusing mainly on basic public infrastructure investments (including rehabilitation of roads, bridges and railroads, health, education, and social protection) and a number of projects in the public utilities, energy, and oil and gas sectors. So far, public investment programs have been established in Kazakhstan and the Kyrgyz Republic; the size of the public investment program in the Kyrgyz Republic exceeded 5 percent of GDP in 1998. In both countries, the public investment programs are financed mainly by foreign borrowing.

Tax Policy and Tax Administration Reforms

As discussed in Section IV, most of the countries in the region have experienced a significant decline in their revenue to GDP ratios. These declines have reflected the well-documented problems experienced by most transition economies—the shrinkage of most traditional tax bases relative to GDP; the problems of adapting tax structures to capture the changing nature of activity and the expanding private sector; and the inefficiencies of tax administrations, including weak compliance with governance requirements of a market economy.[19] Special factors have also prevailed in the region, however, particularly regarding revenue generation from energy sector taxes. For example, payments difficulties for Turkmenistan's gas exports, coupled with a heavy goods component in payments, have severely constrained the ability to raise revenue from the gas sector. Because gas is the largest single source of budget revenue, the country has been hit hard by these developments. Uzbekistan stands out as the only country in the region where the share of the general government sector has remained at over 30 percent of GDP. The durability of revenues reflects, for the most part, the smaller output decline, the less strict budget constraints faced by state enterprises, restrictions on cash withdrawal from banks, and the benefits to tax collections in periods of high inflation in the absence of adjustments to allowances for depreciation and other deductions to enterprise profits.

Tax policy reforms have generally advanced more than tax administration reforms (Table 8.3), albeit with considerable variation across the Central Asian states. Kazakhstan and, to a lesser extent, the Kyrgyz Republic, Tajikistan, and Uzbekistan have made

---

[19]See Hemming, Cheasty, and Lahiri (1995) and Ebrill and Havrylyshyn (1999).

Table 8.3. Summary of Tax Administration Reform

| Country | Legal Framework | | | Organization | |
	Tax adminis-tration law	Legal power for collection	Legal provision for taxpayer rights	Organizational structure	Large taxpayer unit
Kazakhstan	Yes, part of tax code of 1995	Yes, Article 172 of tax code	Yes, Article 142 of tax code	Planned	No
Kyrgyz Republic	Yes, part of tax code	Yes, but court approval required	Implicit in tax code	By taxpayer, but moving to functional	Yes
Tajikistan	Planned	Planned	Planned	Under consideration	Yes, monitoring only
Turkmenistan	No	No	No	Mixed (any type of tax, taxpayer and function)	No, but concentration of large taxpayers in current structure
Uzbekistan	Yes	Yes	Limited	By taxes and regions	Planned

| Country | Planning | | Registration | | Filing |
	Strategic plan	Annual audit plan	Annual taxpayer register	Unique TIN exists	Self-assessment
Kazakhstan	Yes, but priorities not implemented	Partially; action plan specifies priority areas for audit	National register under development	No, only within each rayon	In law, not in practice
Kyrgyz Republic	No	No	Yes, but covers businesses only	Planned	Yes, but limited
Tajikistan	No	No	Planned	Planned	No
Turkmenistan	No	No	Not clear	Planned	Very limited
Uzbekistan	No	Yes, but along traditional lines	Yes	Yes	Limited

| Country | Collection Enforcement | | | |
	Detection of nonregistered taxpayers	Detection of stop filers	Detection of delinquent accounts	Arrears monitoring system
Kazakhstan	No	Only at pilot office	No	Only at pilot office
Kyrgyz Republic	Under development	Yes, but limited	Yes, in process	Yes, but computer system not fully integrated
Tajikistan	No	Not systematic	Not systematic	No
Turkmenistan	Not clear	Not clear	Not clear	Not clear
Uzbekistan	Not systematic	In place	Yes	Yes

Source: Ebrill and Havrylyshyn (1999).

considerable progress in reforming their tax policies. New tax codes were introduced in Kazakhstan (mid-1995), the Kyrgyz Republic (mid-1996), Uzbekistan (January 1998), and Tajikistan (November 1998). Tax reform has just started in Turkmenistan, which essentially retains the systems inherited from the former Soviet Union.

On specific taxes, most progress has been achieved in the elimination of export taxes and excess wage taxes, with mixed progress in the introduction of appropriate value-added tax, excise tax, and personal income tax regimes, and in the unification of rates within various tax categories. Not surprisingly, least progress has taken place on aspects that are very difficult to implement either technically or politically, such as the introduction of new accounting systems and standards, the elimination of exemptions, the consistent use of a destination basis for value-added tax, and the effective taxation of small businesses.[20]

As the transition to a market economy proceeded, the new tax administrations had to shift from handling the taxation of a highly controlled state sector to the more difficult task of ensuring compliance by the emerging private sector and still state-owned but more autonomous enterprises. Tax administration reforms, by their nature, take more time and effort than changes in tax policy itself. It is, therefore, not surprising that progress generally has been slow. Reforms covered enactment of tax administration legislation consistent with the shift to market-oriented economies; management and organizational reforms, including the establishment of large taxpayer units; development of systems and procedures, including audit programs, taxpayer registration procedures, filing and payment procedures, and computerization; and collection, enforcement, and determination of the scope of noncompliance. Table 8.3 provides some indicators of tax administration reform in countries in the region. Kazakhstan again leads the way, with a strong legal framework, and planning and registration arrangements in place. The other countries in the region generally lag behind considerably in each of these fields, and Uzbekistan and Turkmenistan, notably, have no clear plans for reforms.

---

[20]For a detailed description of changes in taxation, see Ebrill and Havrylyshyn (1999).

Bibliography

de Castello Branco, Marta, 1998, "Pension Reform in the Baltics, Russia, and Other Countries of the Former Soviet Union," IMF Working Paper 98/11 (Washington: International Monetary Fund).

Ebrill, Liam, and Oleh Havrylyshyn, 1999, *Tax Reform in the Baltics, Russia, and Other Countries of the Former Soviet Union*, IMF Occasional Paper No. 182 (Washington: International Monetary Fund).

European Bank for Reconstruction and Development, 1996, *Transition Report* (London: EBRD).

———, 1997, *Transition Report* (London: EBRD).

Havrylyshyn, Oleh, Thomas Wolf, Julian Berengaut, Marta de Castello Branco, Ron van Rooden, and Valerie Mercer-Blackman, (forthcoming), *Growth Experience in Transition Countries: 1990–98*, IMF Occasional Paper No. 184 (Washington: International Monetary Fund).

Hemming, Richard, Adrienne Cheasty, and Ashok K. Lahiri, 1995, "The Revenue Decline," in *Policy Experiences and Issues in the Baltics, Russia, and Other Countries of the Former Soviet Union*, Daniel A. Citrin and Ashok K. Lahiri, eds., IMF Occasional Paper No. 133 (Washington: International Monetary Fund).

Hoelscher, David S., 1998, "Banking System Restructuring in Kazakhstan," IMF Working Paper 98/96 (Washington: International Monetary Fund).

Horton, Mark A., 1996, "Health and Education Expenditures in Russia, the Baltic States, and the Other Countries of the Former Soviet Union," IMF Working Paper 96/126 (Washington: International Monetary Fund).

International Monetary Fund, World Bank, Organization for Economic Cooperation and Development, European Bank for Reconstruction and Development, 1991, *A Study of the Soviet Economy*, Vols. 1 and 2 (Washington: International Monetary Fund).

Kemme, David M., and Andrzej Rudka, eds., 1992, *Monetary and Banking Reform in Post Communist Economies: A Special Report*, IEWSS Occasional Paper Series (New York: Institute for East-West Security Studies).

Knight, Malcolm D., and others, 1997, *Central Bank Reforms in the Baltics, Russia, and Other Countries of the Former Soviet Union*, IMF Occasional Paper No. 157 (Washington: International Monetary Fund).

Kornai, János, 1994, "Transformational Recession: The Main Causes," *Journal of Comparative Economics*, Vol. 19 (August), pp. 39–63.

Tait, Alan, 1994, "Budgetary and Tax Reforms, Institutional Requirements, and Fiscal Policy," in *Coordinating Stabilization and Structural Reform,* ed. by Richard C. Barth, Alan R. Roe, and Chorng-Huey Wong, IMF Institute (Washington: International Monetary Fund).

Tanzi, Vito, 1993, "Fiscal Policy and Economic Restructuring of Economies in Transition," IMF Working Paper 93/22 (Washington: International Monetary Fund).

IX   Past Lessons and Future Challenges

Emine Gürgen

The economic reform experiences of the Central Asian states during 1992–98 indicate considerable progress in the region, as a whole, toward establishing a sound macroeconomic environment, but mixed success with structural reforms. Several important lessons can be drawn from the diverse experiences of the five countries in meeting the challenges posed by transition.

- It is clear that the faster reformers—Kazakhstan and the Kyrgyz Republic—have progressed much further than the other three countries in moving toward a market framework and overcoming the inertia of implementing difficult structural measures, with some positive initial results already in evidence.

- The experiences of Kazakhstan and the Kyrgyz Republic illustrate that perseverance with reforms considerably augments their effectiveness and promotes their acceptability. The reform process, once firmly in motion, becomes self-reinforcing and sends the right signals both domestically and abroad.

- While each country in the group is unique, the experiences of Kazakhstan and the Kyrgyz Republic could provide useful guidance to the other three countries, where reform efforts started later and displayed more of a start-stop nature with mixed results, notwithstanding some contributing special factors.

- It is important for all of the countries in the group to ensure that reforms are binding, in the sense that the measures legislated or decreed are actually implemented, so that the changes introduced make a real impact.

- The group, as a whole, could benefit from the experiences of those transition economies inside and outside the region that have weathered similar challenges and considerably advanced their reforms.

For the slower reformers—Tajikistan, Turkmenistan, and Uzbekistan—it will be important to switch from crisis management to a deliberate pursuit of policies aimed at containing macroeconomic imbalances and laying the groundwork for sustainable growth. Such a shift requires the formulation and determined implementation of comprehensive and internally consistent economic stabilization and reform programs. This is already in evidence, to some extent, in Tajikistan. For the countries that are more advanced in their reforms—Kazakhstan and the Kyrgyz Republic—the major challenge will be to avoid re-igniting inflationary and balance of payments pressures through undue easing of fiscal and monetary policies, while at the same time deepening and building upon the structural changes introduced so far. In all of the countries reviewed, the success of the adjustment and reform programs adopted will depend crucially on the extent to which the governments concerned take responsibility for them, as well as on broad endorsement of the programs by influential groups outside of the government.

Essentially, further action is needed in five key areas:

- enhancing the quality of fiscal adjustment;
- strengthening financial intermediation and institutions;
- improving external debt management;
- increasing the depth and scope of structural reforms; and
- addressing governance and corruption issues.

These areas are briefly discussed and the policy implications are outlined below.

In the Central Asian states, as in most other transition economies, the brunt of fiscal adjustment has, thus far, mostly been borne by expenditure cuts and/or arrears, with insufficient attention paid to the level and quality of government expenditure on social services (notably health and education), basic infrastructure, and operations and maintenance. Efforts to raise revenue have been thwarted by tax administrations that are ill equipped to enforce tax collections, the prevalence of domestic payments arrears (including by governments), and flourishing underground economies that largely escape taxation. Future efforts will need to be directed at considerably raising tax revenue collections—which will also benefit from the strengthening of the economic recoveries under way—and better prioritizing of expenditure, including through civil service reforms, the curtailment of nonproductive spending, and the adoption of public investment programs. Progress in these areas will be the most effective way of avoiding the recurrence of payments arrears in these countries, and of dismantling the widespread system of mutually offsetting expenditure and tax arrears, which has further weakened payments discipline and reduced the transparency of government operations. Also, as reforms take hold and many of the present distortions arising from a mixture of controls and liberal policies are removed, underground economies can be expected to shrink, allowing for more effective and equitable taxation.

Notwithstanding some cross-country differences, the banking systems of the Central Asian states are still at a fairly elementary stage of development, with considerable further scope for institutional strengthening and improvements in banking practices. A few large state banks continue to account for the bulk of transactions, acting more as agents of the state than independent financial intermediaries. An important task ahead for these countries will be to restructure their banking systems with a view toward strengthening the effectiveness of monetary policy and supporting the economic recoveries already under way. Action in this area will also be needed to safeguard against protracted structural lending to bail out failing banks and enterprises, arrest currency substitution, and promote an efficient and solvent banking system. Such action will entail improving the functioning of legal and accounting frameworks, adopting effective prudential regulations, and strengthening bank supervision. While the countries in the group have made considerable progress in these areas with technical assistance from abroad, more needs to be accomplished to enhance public confidence in the financial systems and to align the systems closely with the needs of a modern market economy.

External borrowing by the Central Asian states has grown rapidly during the period reviewed, primarily to finance budget deficits, meet growing import bills, and benefit from a cheaper source of finance, given the large differentials between foreign and domestic interest rates that were not fully offset by exchange rate depreciations. For the most part, borrowing strategies were formulated on the basis of short-term considerations, with insufficient attention to medium-term debt sustainability issues. The funds borrowed were, therefore, not always channeled to uses that would generate the earnings needed to service the debt. The institutional arrangements for the management and monitoring of the external debt,

moreover, were generally weak and not clear. Given these shortcomings and the risk that excessive reliance on foreign borrowing could postpone fiscal and structural reforms and trigger debt-servicing difficulties, the Central Asian states need to keep their borrowing strategies under close review, formulate such strategies within a medium-term framework, and strengthen the institutional arrangements for external debt management and monitoring. They need to keep in mind, moreover, that benefits from official and private capital inflows will be greater to the extent that such funds are channeled toward productive investment.

While all Central Asian states have begun implementing structural reforms, the depth and determination with which this has been done has varied considerably across countries. For the slower reformers, it will be essential to give priority to catching up in key areas such as privatization and enterprise restructuring. For those countries that have made substantive progress in these areas, the next stage might usefully be to extend their efforts to reforming the labor market, the civil service, and the trade and regulatory systems, while also more aggressively pursuing sectoral (notably agrarian) reforms. At the same time, to strengthen the confidence of private savers and investors, continued modification of state intervention in economic activity will be needed. This can best be achieved by limiting the functions of the state essentially to the provision of reliable public services, the establishment of a simple and transparent regulatory framework, and the enforcement of property rights and a fair judicial system.

Finally, firmly tackling governance and corruption issues will be an important challenge for the Central Asian states, where such problems have frequently arisen, as it has in many other transition economies. There is considerable empirical evidence that corruption, or the abuse of public power for private benefit, is harmful to sound economic performance because it tends to be associated with lower investment, reduced economic growth, concentration of government spending on less productive activities, and a greater incidence of income inequality and poverty.[1] The most effective way of dealing with governance and corruption issues lies in structural, institutional, and legal reforms. Such reforms, by better balancing the roles of the state and market and clearly establishing the rules of law, can be expected to limit the conditions that breed corruption, promote private sector activity, and help restore confidence that is essential to attracting foreign capital needed to strengthen the economic recoveries under way in the Central Asian states.

---

[1]See Abed (1998), and Tanzi (1998).

Bibliography

Abed, George T., 1998, "Governance Issues and Transition Economies," paper presented at the international conference cosponsored by the Kyrgyz Republic and the International Monetary Fund in honor of the fifth anniversary of the Kyrgyz som, "Challenges to Economies in Transition: Stabilization, Growth, and Governance," Bishkek, May.

Knight, Malcolm D., and others, 1997, *Central Bank Reforms in the Baltics, Russia, and Other Countries of the Former Soviet Union*, IMF Occasional Paper No. 157 (Washington: International Monetary Fund).

Kopits, George, and Jon Craig, 1998, *Transparency in Government Operations*, IMF Occasional Paper No. 158 (Washington: International Monetary Fund).

Odling-Smee, John, and Basil Zavoico, 1998, "External Borrowing in the Baltics, Russia, and Other States of the Former Soviet Union: The Transition to a Market Economy," IMF Paper on Policy Analysis and Assessment 98/5 (Washington: International Monetary Fund).

Tanzi, Vito, 1998, "Corruption Around the World: Causes, Consequences, Scope, and Cures," *IMF Staff Papers*, International Monetary Fund, Vol. 45 (December), pp. 559–94.

Recent Occasional Papers of the International Monetary Fund

161. The Nordic Banking Crises: Pitfalls in Financial Liberalization? by Burkhard Dress and Ceyla Pazarbaşıoğlu. 1998.

160. Fiscal Reform in Low-Income Countries: Experience Under IMF-Supported Programs, by a staff team led by George T. Abed and comprising Liam Ebrill, Sanjeev Gupta, Benedict Clements, Ronald Mc-Morran, Anthony Pellechio, Jerald Schiff, and Marijn Verhoeven. 1998.

159. Hungary: Economic Policies for Sustainable Growth, Carlo Cottarelli, Thomas Krueger, Reza Moghadam, Perry Perone, Edgardo Ruggiero, and Rachel van Elkan. 1998.

158. Transparency in Government Operations, by George Kopits and Jon Craig. 1998.

157. Central Bank Reforms in the Baltics, Russia, and the Other Countries of the Former Soviet Union, by a staff team led by Malcolm Knight and comprising Susana Almuiña, John Dalton, Inci Otker, Ceyla Pazarbaşıoğlu, Arne B. Petersen, Peter Quirk, Nicholas M. Roberts, Gabriel Sensenbrenner, and Jan Willem van der Vossen. 1997.

156. The ESAF at Ten Years: Economic Adjustment and Reform in Low-Income Countries, by the staff of the International Monetary Fund. 1997.

155. Fiscal Policy Issues During the Transition in Russia, by Augusto Lopez-Claros and Sergei V. Alexas-henko. 1998.

154. Credibility Without Rules? Monetary Frameworks in the Post–Bretton Woods Era, by Carlo Cottarelli and Curzio Giannini. 1997.

153. Pension Regimes and Saving, by G.A. Mackenzie, Philip Gerson, and Alfredo Cuevas. 1997.

152. Hong Kong, China: Growth, Structural Change, and Economic Stability During the Transition, by John Dodsworth and Dubravko Mihaljek. 1997.

151. Currency Board Arrangements: Issues and Experiences, by a staff team led by Tomás J.T. Baliño and Charles Enoch. 1997.

150. Kuwait: From Reconstruction to Accumulation for Future Generations, by Nigel Andrew Chalk, Mohamed A. El-Erian, Susan J. Fennell, Alexei P. Kireyev, and John F. Wilson. 1997.

149. The Composition of Fiscal Adjustment and Growth: Lessons from Fiscal Reforms in Eight Economies, by G.A. Mackenzie, David W.H. Orsmond, and Philip R. Gerson. 1997.

148. Nigeria: Experience with Structural Adjustment, by Gary Moser, Scott Rogers, and Reinold van Til, with Robin Kibuka and Inutu Lukonga. 1997.

147. Aging Populations and Public Pension Schemes, by Sheetal K. Chand and Albert Jaeger. 1996.

146. Thailand: The Road to Sustained Growth, by Kalpana Kochhar, Louis Dicks-Mireaux, Balazs Horvath, Mauro Mecagni, Erik Offerdal, and Jianping Zhou. 1996.

145. Exchange Rate Movements and Their Impact on Trade and Investment in the APEC Region, by Takatoshi Ito, Peter Isard, Steven Symansky, and Tamim Bayoumi. 1996.

144. National Bank of Poland: The Road to Indirect Instruments, by Piero Ugolini. 1996.

143. Adjustment for Growth: The African Experience, by Michael T. Hadjimichael, Michael Nowak, Robert Sharer, and Amor Tahari. 1996.

142. Quasi-Fiscal Operations of Public Financial Institutions, by G.A. Mackenzie and Peter Stella. 1996.

141. Monetary and Exchange System Reforms in China: An Experiment in Gradualism, by Hassanali Mehran, Marc Quintyn, Tom Nordman, and Bernard Laurens. 1996.

140. Government Reform in New Zealand, by Graham C. Scott. 1996.

139. Reinvigorating Growth in Developing Countries: Lessons from Adjustment Policies in Eight Economies, by David Goldsbrough, Sharmini Coorey, Louis Dicks-Mireaux, Balazs Horvath, Kalpana Kochhar, Mauro Mecagni, Erik Offerdal, and Jianping Zhou. 1996.

138. Aftermath of the CFA Franc Devaluation, by Jean A.P. Clément, with Johannes Mueller, Stéphane Cossé, and Jean Le Dem. 1996.

Note: For information on the title and availability of Occasional Papers not listed, please consult the IMF Publications Catalog or contact IMF Publication Services.